The Wealth of the World

The Proven Wealth Transfer System

By
John Avanzini

HARRISON HOUSE
Tulsa, Oklahoma

Wealth of the World
The Proven Wealth Transfer System
ISBN 0-89274-580-0
Copyright © 1989 by
Dr. John Avanzini
Box 1057
Hurst, Texas 76053

Published by Harrison House, Inc.
P. O. Box 35035
Tulsa, OK 74153

Contents

Dedication

Lovingly dedicated to my firstborn son,
Mr. Tony Marcel Avanzini
"Truly a Gentle Man of God"

Foreword

How many times have you turned the television channel when the business segment of the news came on? Have you ever skipped the business section of the newspaper without even reading the headlines? I am sure we all have. But for many of you readers, it is time that you started paying more careful attention to what is going on in these arenas because some of you are going to be controlling them — soon.

Consider some facts about three key markets in the world economy today. Keep in mind that these statistics pertain largely to the private sector (as opposed to governments), so they refer to actions taken by companies owned by individuals. Perhaps you did not know that. . .

* There was an average of $5.4 billion in transactions per day on the New York Stock Exchange during July 1986.

* There averaged more than $484 billion worth of foreign currency transactions per day with financial institutions in the U.S. during March 1986.

* U.S. corporations recently raised more than $25 billion in cash in the Eurobond market in less than six months.

A staggering amount of wealth is stockpiled in the world today. Furthermore, the technology to accumulate much more also exists. However, most of the wealth in the world is controlled by less than ten percent of the population. That is why it should not surprise us that intense poverty, malnutrition and inadequate housing plague much of our planet.

Poverty is not God's best. Lack is not in God's plan for His people. God has emphasized repeatedly in His Word that He wants to meet our every need (Phil. 4:19), and He wants us to live the abundant life (John 10:10). But in order to live the abundant life in the physical realm, we as individuals, and more importantly as the Body of Christ, must be able to obtain and accumulate wealth like the corporate sections of the U.S., Japan and the other industrial powers of the world. But how can we do this?

God has said in His Word that He has given *you* the power to get wealth (Deut. 8:18). In fact, if the numbers quoted above seem large, be advised that God is able to do exceeding abundantly above all we can ask or think (Eph. 3:10). Yes, we as individuals, and as the Body of Christ, will control more wealth and power than most of us can currently imagine. But for what purpose? How? When?

God is preparing some of you right now to be among the men and women He will use in the miraculous end-time harvest of souls and wealth. But you must know and understand His plan. He has revealed it and has explained it in His Word. Dr. John Avanzini has prepared a careful teaching based entirely on God's Word to help you prepare for your part in this harvest. See what God has in store for *The Wealth of the World.*

Professor Eugene Flood, Jr.
Assistant Professor of Finance
Stanford University
Graduate School of Business

Introduction

> A good man leaveth an inheritance to his children's children: and *the wealth of the sinner is laid up for the just.*
>
> Proverbs 13:22

> He that by usury and unjust gain increaseth his substance, *he shall gather it for him that will pity the poor.*
>
> Proverbs 28:8

> For God giveth to a man that is good in his sight wisdom, and knowledge, and joy: but to the sinner he giveth travail, *to gather and to heap up, that he may give to him that is good before God....*
>
> Ecclesiastes 2:26

> Though he heap up silver as the dust, and prepare raiment as the clay; He may prepare it, but the just shall put it on, and *the innocent shall divide the silver.*
>
> Job 27:16,17

This book contains vital, spiritual information that is of the utmost importance to all Christians in these Endtimes.

As you and other Christians around the world reading this book begin to fully comprehend the Biblical concepts contained in these pages, I honestly believe *the very course of our world will be significantly altered,* both materially and spiritually!

Christian global satellite networks will span the entire world. Powerful Christian television stations will beam Christian programming twenty-four hours a day to every hamlet, city, and metropolis in the world.

Bibles will be in virtually every home, everywhere in the world. Well-used Bibles will be displayed in corporate board rooms throughout the globe.

Christian churches will be on virtually every corner, filled to capacity, with multiple services, and *the entire global Body of Christ will be nourished with the knowledge of God's Word.*

I am convinced that God has shown me a world-changing revelation directly from His Word. In this book, I will document, line upon line, precept upon precept from the Word of God, a clear prophecy that shows there will soon be a dramatic transfer of the world's wealth, literally ripping the world's wealth from the control of the wicked and placing it into the hands of God's informed people everywhere.

These select, informed, endtime people will direct these riches into the hands of Christian churches and God-honoring ministries to use to finance God's endtime, global, revival harvest that is now ripe for the reaping.

I will prove from Scripture that this miraculous transfer of wealth will most surely take place during these last days, when God will begin giving to the prepared Christians every, single financial blessing needed to properly and expeditiously bring in this already ripe endtime harvest.

My own careful, painstaking, meticulous study of the Scripture, combined with my prayerful seeking for revelation in this matter through the Holy Spirit, has led me to understand that God is going to literally confiscate the gold, the silver, the stocks, the bonds, virtually every form of wealth that the wicked possess and *in these last days, transfer that wealth to the "just"* (*dedicated, informed, committed Christians*) *to properly and abundantly fund the final events in His endtime plan.*

As incredible as it may sound: The gold in Fort Knox could belong to the Christians. The stocks on the stock exchange could be primarily bought and sold, and literally controlled by Christians. The oil wealth once dominated by OPEC, the diamond wealth of Africa, the plutonium wealth of Russia, the technical wealth of Japan, *all* of these *and more,* could be at the disposal of and in the possession of Christians who would carefully dedicate it to finance the Kingdom of God!

It is not very difficult for me to guess your first reactions to this possibility. I can almost hear you saying, "Brother John, you have flipped your lid! Can you possibly know what you are claiming? I've never heard anything so crazy, so ridiculous, so foolish in all my life! Frankly, this sounds like a fantastic story from way out in left field."

Yes, I *do* admit the statements I have just made about the world's wealth being transferred to the Christians *are* shocking.

Yes, they *do* sound crazy. Yes, they *do* seem ridiculous. Yes, the statements *appear* unfounded and foolish.

But, remember who we are dealing with. He is the great God Jehovah who has clearly stated in His Word His unconventional nature and His revolutionary approach to all of mankind's affairs.

> **For my thoughts are not your thoughts, neither are your ways my ways, saith the Lord.**
> **Isaiah 55:8**

So please consider your position and test whether the spirit-led interpretations of the Biblical principles contained in this book are correct. Even if the principles sound strange to you, please put aside your preconceived ideas and consider the principles. Don't place yourself in the position of missing being a part of this very important endtime revelation.

Think back. Your preconceived ideas have not always immediately meshed with the deep truth of God's Word.

Pause a moment before making any final decisions on this matter: think about it. Just how did you feel the first time you heard about Jonah and the whale?

Did you, without an argument whatsoever from your natural mind, blindly accept the virgin birth the first time you heard about God's plan for Mary?

Wasn't the same spirit of doubt around the first time you heard that the huge walls of Jericho came tumbling down by the trampling of feet, a shout, and a sequence of trumpet blasts?

Child of God, it is commonplace for the things of God to confound the wise!

It is very possible that you may have never before heard the truths contained in this book! Therefore, I suggest that *before* you decide these concepts are *crazy*, *before* you decide these teachings are *foolish*, *before* you term this book as "heresy," please *carefully consider the sacred evidence* from the Word of God, and from your God-given unction of the Holy Spirit that has been placed in you by the new birth.

Then *you* be the judge.

Prayerfully consider the distinct possibility that what God has shown me is indeed revelation and a key endtime prophecy. If you do this, then this book will have a dramatic effect upon your life, and upon the part that you will have in God's final endtime harvest.

As a serious Christian concerned about God's final endtime harvest, I pray you will carefully weigh the Scriptural evidence in this book and give it your most serious, spiritual attention.

Remember, the saint who has "an ear to hear and eyes to see" has the privilege of riding on the cutting edge of God's present truth.

I do pray that you will be able to take a lesson from slumbering Israel who could not see through her blind eyes and could not hear with her heavy ears. Remember, it was because of her preconceived ideas about the first coming of the Messiah that she missed her visitation and totally misinterpreted the first advent of our Lord and Savior, Jesus Christ. Israel's reason for missing the Messiah was simply stated by our Lord that she could not discern the time.

> **Ye hypocrites, ye can discern the face of the sky and of the earth; but *how is it that ye do not discern this time?***
>
> **Luke 12:56**

God has no surprises for His saints who are willing to discern the time, for God has said He will do nothing in the earth unless He first notifies His prophets, who in turn inform His people:

13

Surely the Lord God will do nothing, but he revealeth his secret unto his servants the prophets.
Amos 3:7

My prayer for you today is that you will not be as the foolish virgins and arrive at the midnight hour of this age without oil for the lamps of the Gospel that will illuminate the whole world in these last days.

1

The Battle Plan of Satan: Containment

Child of God, I alert you to the fact that Satan is clearly waging a battle of containment against the saints of God.

He is not nearly as concerned with driving you backwards as he is with *containing* you where you are, and keeping you from getting where God wants you to go.

Can you identify with that?

In your prayer life, if you desire a greater walk with God, you will find that the devil will let you continue to pray at your current prayer level. But as soon as you try to break into a new dimension of prayer, frequent distractions occur.

People come to visit you. Your hours will change at work. The phone will ring. Any time you start to move decisively forward, Satan increases the *battle of containment.*

You may have experienced this battle of containment in the realm of holiness or sanctification. You achieve a certain walk, then all of a sudden, you stop growing. You do not especially go backwards, but you just find it increasingly difficult to move forward.

Child of God, *that* is the stark reality of Satan's battle of containment against you!

As you start to grow in the revelations I am bringing to you in this book, you will quickly realize that at this very moment the devil is waging a powerful battle of containment in your finances.

He will tell you that *you are getting along okay, so just don't rock the boat!*

He will even try to deceive you into thinking that this book is *just another prosperity message, but do not be distracted!*

Please recognize that this is the *vital Biblical message* of deliverance from the ever-present insufficiency that your spirit man has been hungering after!

Do not let the devil continue to contain you in your present financial dilemma!

One of the primary deceptions that so many Christians have been deceived into thinking is that the Bible says, "*the truth will set you free.*"

The Bible does not say that the truth will set you free. What the Bible says is something very different. Read carefully now what it actually says:

> **And ye shall *know* the truth, and the truth shall make you free.**
>
> **John 8:32**

Do you see it? It is *the truth that you know* that has the divine power to set you free. Please hear me. The only truth that can set you free is the truth *that you personally know.* You can walk around with the truth (the Bible) in your right hand, placed lovingly over your breast; you can walk around with that precious Bible right over your lungs, and still have a horrible cancer

16

grow in those lungs that will eventually snuff out your very life.

Most Christians die prematurely in the presence of truth, with the Bible on the nightstand next to their death bed. But child of God, keep this in mind. The *presence* of truth cannot and does not heal! You see, it is not the presence of truth, but *the knowledge* of truth that has power and sets you free. Hear the Scriptures well:

> **And ye shall *know* the truth, and the truth shall make you free.**
> **John 8:32**

It is time to order our lives line upon line, precept upon precept, concept upon Biblical concept. We must build a foundation of truth so powerful that Satan cannot contain it.

Now hear me well, child of God. I want you to break out of the containment building that Satan has constructed around your finances.

Please, be very careful, and do not mistake *a mere penetration* of Satan's containment in your finances *as a breakthrough*. There is a vast difference between a penetration and a breakthrough, and I want nothing less for you from this book than a *total breakthrough!*

Perhaps you have made an occasional penetration in the wall of containment Satan has placed around your finances. Maybe you have already gained enough bits and pieces of knowledge to understand that God does not intend for you to be poor, and that He has a Biblical plan of abundance for your life.

I want you to go beyond bits and pieces. It is time for you to start gathering *great quantities* of spiritual power. When this power is complete, it will bring about a *total breakthrough* in your finances which will move you permanently beyond Satan's containment!

Remember, any time you break through a spiritual barrier, *it takes great spiritual energy*; it takes the power of God working through you!

Without a doubt, it is the most potent type of power in the universe. As you understand the *truth* of this powerful revelation, as you *know* this truth by putting it into *practical application* in your life, you will experience a powerful new day in your finances, a true and lasting spiritual breakthrough.

Surely you have experienced the *difference* between penetration and breakthrough in your own life.

Remember when you first heard about sanctification? As you began to gather bits and pieces of Biblical truth on this subject, your spiritual energy level rose until finally you had enough spiritual power for a penetration. How wonderful the land of sanctification, beyond Satan's wall of containment, looked. Remember how you peered through the hole in that wall and said, "Look how wonderfully sanctified my life could be if I could only break through this wall of containment?"

The breakthrough only came when you allowed that energy, that input of Biblical truth, to continue and continue to grow. It took effort. It literally took a violent effort, not casual daydreaming and wishing, to accomplish it.

The same energy that brought you your previous breakthrough, the same level of effort that swept you to past victories, must now come forth for you to achieve a financial breakthrough as you are guided by this book. You must *gather* many Biblical principles relating to the financing of God's endtime harvest, and then *apply* these principles today and tomorrow. Not so you can make just a little hole and peer through a small, rapidly closing penetration, but so you can achieve nothing less than a *total breakthrough*!

Satan has contained you in your finances long enough! Jericho's walls must come down!

If there is still any doubt that Satan is containing you in your finances, let me quickly prove to you that he is.

Right now, you can think of several people who are not as smart nor as qualified as you are who are making more money than you make. How can this be unless the devil has put an invisible wall around your financial potential? You see, the devil does not care how much money non-Christians make, because as long as they control it, their money will not be used to finance the preaching of the Gospel to those who have not yet heard the message of Jesus Christ.

The rock stars will never finance the gospel. The raunchy movie producers will not give one dime for the next major evangelistic crusade.

That's why the devil does not contain them like he does you and me! You see, financing the endtime harvest is up to you and me as born-again Christians. If you do not have the financial breakthrough God wants you to have, His Church will never rise to the full level of the vision that God has for it.

That's why Satan wants to contain you in your current financial strata. You know I am telling the truth. If you make $200 extra one month, he sees to it that the tire will blow out on your car, or the water heater will go out at your home.

Don't you see, it is the devil who wages this continual battle of containment against your finances?

Every time you try to enter into a financial breakthrough, he will come against you, and the only way to smash and destroy the wall of containment around your finances is through a violent, highly energetic act on your part.

Child of God, I don't use the word "violent" at my choosing, but God's Word tells us to literally get violent and use our God-given force (spiritual energy).

> **And from the days of John the Baptist until now the kingdom of heaven suffereth violence, and *the violent take it by force.***
> **Matthew 11:12**

If you want to make a breakthrough in your finances, then determine right now in your mind that you are going to take *whatever action is necessary* to crush the devil's wall of containment around your finances, removing the limitations of that invisible wall and breaking through, by force and violence, into a new level of understanding *and* knowledge in the area of your finances.

You probably already have much spiritual energy from God's Word in you. This book will put even more and more of that spiritual energy into you through a better and broader understanding of His Word.

All of a sudden, you will realize that His Word is concentrated so strongly in you that you now have enough spiritual energy to come with *violent spiritual force* against the invisible wall that is resisting you and pushing against your finances and blow those walls asunder!

You will charge forth into newly discovered wealth and prosperity, *receiving literally more than enough* to help finance every worthwhile Christian ministry that God directs you to help.

I think that you can now see that if you really want this financial breakthrough, it will take more than a penetration. Most of the teaching on finances today only takes you to a point of penetration. Although you have hungered for this breakthrough, you probably never have possessed enough of the spiritual power, the concentrated energy, to break forth and walk out of those satanic walls of containment, into true Biblical financial success and freedom.

Child of God, you are at a critical point!

Now is the time for *your* breakthrough! Read. Study. Absorb. Then take *violent action!*

Begin to seize the financial power that you have according to the Word of God!

2

Your God-Given Power To Get Wealth

"Why is violent action necessary?" you might ask.

You see, those old teachings, those old traditions have made ineffective the Word of God and your Heavenly Father's desire for you to abound. Deuteronomy 8:18a is a good example:

> **But thou shalt remember the Lord thy God: for it is he that giveth thee** *power to get wealth....*

When was the last time you heard anyone give a sermon on *that* Scripture? You see, there are walls around those Scriptures containing the Body of Christ's financial advancement and expansion.

Many of you were brought up in a day when poverty was erroneously deemed by well-meaning preachers and teachers to be glorious and Godly! Unfortunately, the "poverty is holy" doctrine still hangs around in the back of your mind today. Many of you *still believe* there is something wrong with a man who has a lot of money.

I used to think,"Oh God, if I just had enough. Lord, just give me enough to provide for my wife, Pat, and our kids."

Have you ever prayed a prayer like that? Sure you have, but don't ever pray it again!

As this book progresses, I will show you that it is impossible for you to be *the Christian God intends for you to be* with "just enough."

Think about the day you got saved. Your salvation was absolutely free. It did not cost you one penny to get saved. I remember walking into the First Baptist Church of Largo, Florida. They treated me like a king. There was not a charge for anything. My salvation did not cost me one cent.

But after I got saved, when I came back the next Wednesday night, and from that day on, I have been handing out money everywhere I go!

Child of God, do you understand what I am talking about here? It costs money to bring in God's harvest, and the Church of our Lord and Savior will never have enough to do it as long as saints have *"just enough."* We can bring in the endtime harvest only if God's saints learn how to have *more than enough* to supply the funds needed to do the great work that God has put before us.

Let's begin generating some spiritual energy in the area of your finances. Let's begin right now by destroying one old concept that must go from your mind before you can move any further in your finances.

Child of God, establish this new thought in your mind:

There is nothing wrong with me and my family living the good life!

It is God's portion for me.

> **Behold that which I have seen: it is good and comely for one to eat and to drink, and** *to enjoy the good of all of his labour* **that he taketh under the sun all the days of his life, which God giveth him:** *for it is his portion.*
>
> **Every man also to whom God hath given** *riches* **and** *wealth,* **and hath given him power to eat thereof, and** *to take his portion,* **and to rejoice in his labour;** *this is the gift of God.*
>
> **Ecclesiastes 5:18,19**

The good life is your portion!

Most Christians get it in their minds that there is great insufficiency in the world, and that we must live all of our lives in that insufficiency.

Child of God, let me assure you, that is not God's way. He says, "There is more than enough." He says, "The good life is your portion!"

Do you see how Satan is waging a battle in your mind, a battle of containment? It is hard for many to grasp just "having enough," let alone grasping that God intends for you to have *more than enough.*

Remember, it is the world's method to have its population operate in insufficiency, shortage, and want. They feel that's the way to keep prices up, through contrived, manipulated shortage!

But do not forget, we are not of this world, and our God and King declares that the basis of His Kingdom is *abundance!* He plainly says:

> **. . . I am come that they might have life, and that they might have it** *more abundantly.*
>
> **John 10:10b**

You see, the lifestyle God has chosen for us *is* His abundance. This abundant lifestyle is the type of a breakthrough that you are heading for if you do not let the devil contain you in your current strata of income — through distraction, ringing phones, and other devices — to get you away from *knowing* the truth of God's Word that I am trying to teach you.

Oh, saint of God, press on, and you will stomp on the devil. God says the devil will soon be bruised under your feet:

> **And the God of peace shall bruise Satan under your feet shortly.**
>
> **Romans 16:20a**

Notice the last portion of Ecclesiastes 5:19 says that the good life is your portion, it is "the gift of God," and you have the power to eat your portion.

I can just hear some of you saying, "Well, Brother John, if wealth and the good life are God's gifts to me, then why don't I have them?"

If you know anything about God, you know that God does not hand out all of His gifts on a silver platter. A good illustration of God's nature is seen when He "gave" the promised land to Israel. It was a gift, but they had to *violently fight* to receive it. There was not one square foot that came easily, yet Scripture clearly states it was God's gift to them. God has set aside a portion of the world's wealth for you. It is yours for the taking. But to take control of that wealth involves your decision to *violently fight* and take it out of the control of God's enemies, just as Israel took the promised land from the enemies of God. (Please notice that this fight is in the spirit world. I am not advocating an armed conflict.)

Notice through this personal illustration how important it is to know the truth if you expect to be set free by that truth.

In my early ministry, I was Dr. John Avanzini, pastor of First Bible Baptist Church of El Cajon, California. I was a fundamental Baptist, if you please, as narrow-minded as they come. I was so narrow-minded in my view of Scripture and my denomination being right about every single doctrine that I could look through a keyhole with both eyes!

In those early ministry years, when I walked into a hospital, it was like the hospital was having a visit from the angel of death. I would place my hands on a man with a common cold and it would quickly turn into double pneumonia. When I went into the cardiac ward, the Intensive Care nurses would panic.

"Here comes Dr. Avanzini," they would cry. Then, those heart machines that normally go "beep, beep, beep" would start going crazy, and just go "beeeeeeeeeeeeep."

Child of God, are you grasping what I am saying?

I did not *know* that the stripes Jesus received on my behalf and on the behalf of the world had given me *power* to lay hands on the sick and that they would have to recover.

You see, you cannot walk in a truth you do not *know*. Oh, I bought my study books in a bookstore where people knew that truth. I personally was around the truth every day. I earned a doctorate at the Baptist Theological Seminary in Shreveport, Louisiana. But I didn't *know* about the fullness of the Holy Ghost.

You cannot have the full benefit of a truth unless you *know* it. Finally, one day I had a breakthrough. I discovered that the Bible says, *and means*, that I could, right now in the twentieth century, lay hands on the sick and they would recover!

> . . .They shall lay hands on the sick, and they shall recover.
>
> **Mark 16:18b**

Pain just left people when I prayed for them. Symptoms vanished. Terminal cases were healed with a touch — one such case with just a word from the pulpit to a man diagnosed terminal.

I experienced the difference between head knowledge and heart knowledge, the difference between *logos* and *rhema*. Logos is the written Word, but *rhema* is the Word of God *living* in you!

Suddenly, a whole new flow began for me! Wisdom came to me. Healing functioned through me. Once I really *knew* the truth, then I could operate in it.

Right now, you may be powerless in the area of your finances. You may be the victim of your environment which taught you that "poverty is Godly," and which has brought about a poverty atmosphere around you.

Begin now to chisel at those old, false concepts. Start this minute to begin receiving more of your financial breakthrough by absorbing the *rhema* of this incredible Scripture:

> **But thou shalt remember the Lord thy God: for it is he that giveth thee** [that means you] **power to get wealth. . . .**
>
> **Deuteronomy 8:18a**

Read that Scripture out loud several times right now. You have very possibly never read anything like it before. It goes against so much of what you have been taught. But there it is in your Bible, staring at you. Child of God, your breakthrough cannot come unless you cooperate by *violently* pressing against the restraints of Satan that make you question the validity of this Word from God. Read it again and again.

God Himself has given *you* the *power to get wealth!* Isn't that amazing?

You have the power to get wealth, and that power has been given to you by God. Say it out loud: "I have been given the power to get wealth by the God of heaven."

Say it ten times. Say it with confidence. Listen to yourself saying it. If God says this about you, then you can say it about yourself. For the rest of your life, say this to yourself several times each day: *"God has given me the power to get wealth."*

First, receive the *logos* of this statement, the written word; it *is* written in your Holy Bible.

Next, receive the *rhema* of this statement by beginning to *operate* that word in your life.

To *operate* the *rhema* of this statement, you must understand the total context of the verse. *This is very important. Do not miss a word.*

This revelation is more than the "Cadillac Faith" prosperity being taught in so many messages on finances. Although that message is based in a partial truth — it does not go far enough. God does not mind the saints driving Cadillacs, Lincolns, or Hondas. But if that's all the message you hear, then you've totally missed God!

You have thrown away *the pearl* and kept the oyster shell. Let me tell you a story about such a situation.

There was a man who had been listening to the tapes of a certain prosperity preacher, and he was all excited about God making him rich — real quick.

One day he drove up to the church in a big, beautiful new luxury car, and parked it right in the front of the building in the most conspicuous parking space. The preacher, seeing him pull up, asked him, "Where did you get such a nice car?" to which the man replied, "Preacher, God gave me that car."

The preacher congratulated the man, and agreed with him, saying, "That looks like the kind of car God would give."

As they both walked all around the car, the preacher noticed the man's special, personalized license plate. It read, "PRAYED 4."

For the next ten to twelve months, everything seemed just great. Every Sunday, this seemingly prosperous fellow would drive up to the church in his big, beautiful luxury car that was now affectionately being called "Old PRAYED 4." His seeming success caused everyone to feel very envious, and even somewhat convicted that their faith for wealth was not at this man's level.

But one Sunday, here came this same man, not in his luxury car, but this time in, of all things, an old Nash automobile. You remember how they looked. They resembled an upside-down bathtub with the windshield in the blunt end. Well, he slowly drove up in this old car and parked way in the back of the church parking lot in the most obscure parking space.

The preacher, seeing this obvious deviation from what had become his normal entrance, went over to this fellow, and asked, "Hey, where's 'Old PRAYED 4'?"

He said, "Pastor, they repossessed it, and everything else I own is in bankruptcy."

Child of God, can you imagine, they repossessed the car God had supposedly given him! Here we see the all too common end to the "get riches for your own benefit" gospel: disappointment and loss of credibility and our own loss of witness for Christ.

The preacher of our story then put his arms around this fellow and lovingly told him, "Brother, listen to me carefully. I thank God for the teachers we have in our land. But man, you are obviously missing it. Come on into God's house today and start hearing what God really says about your finances, and how they relate to *His purposes,* and not how they relate to *your* purposes. Start learning the prosperity message in the proper context.

"If your motive for giving is right with God, and if you really *know* God's intentions for the prosperity you receive from Him, *then* if you still desire a nice car, God will give it to you. God does not mind you having a nice car, if that is what you really want. And this time, when He gives it to you, it will be better than your last car, and you won't have to have some goofy license plate like 'PRAYED 4' on it. With the car that God gives, you can have a *real* license plate, one that says 'PAID 4.' "

Child of God, begin to hear me on this. Deuteronomy 8:18 tells you that God has given you the *power* to get wealth. But read the verse *in context* and you will see *why* God is giving you that power!

> . . . that he may establish his covenant which he sware unto thy fathers, as it is this day.
> **Deuteronomy 8:18b**

God has given you power to get wealth so that His covenant can be established. The word *established* here means "founded and grounded" financially so that no economic problems could ever uproot or overthrow the orderly operation of that covenant on the earth.

Do you really think that God wants the state of the national or local economy to affect the operation of His Church and His chosen ministries?

Do you really think that God would want every economic slump in the natural realm to disrupt the ministry of His Church? *Of course not!*

Do you understand? God has a plan for His Church (the saints) to be so grounded, so established in finances that literally no problem in the economy will affect the Church's economy: Good times, bad times, depression, recession, it makes no difference. God intends for His Church to grow and flourish, no matter what the world might be facing in its godless economics.

God has given every one of His children the *power* to get wealth so that they can be established financially to generously fund every need that arises for the operation of the covenant He made with Abraham.

That alone is the primary reason why the saints have been given the power to get wealth!

If you are seeking *first* the Kingdom of God and His righteousness, if you are using your God-given power to get wealth to establish God's Kingdom first, *then* the secondary portion of the covenant comes into play, which is adding all of these other things (your needs and wants) unto you.

> **But seek ye first the kingdom of God, and his righteousness; and *all these things* shall be added unto you.**
>
> **Matthew 6:33**

Notice *God* adds "all these things." When you effectively do *your part* of first *establishing His kingdom*, then God will do *His part* — and give you "all these things" you need and want for the good life *in abundance!*

3

You May Have
the Whole Thing Backwards!

Several years ago, a lady in the church I then pastored approached me in the hallway. Rushing towards me with excitement, she could barely contain her beaming smile as she told me, "Brother John, guess what? My husband and I are going to give the Kenneth Copeland ministry a brand-new Lear jet!"

Well, that sounded pretty spectacular to me so I said, "Well, praise God! What a worthwhile ministry to give to." But I must confess that secretly, in my inner mind, I was thinking that since she was going to give Ken Copeland a Lear jet, and she had never even met him — she had only seen him on television — imagine the gift she must have in mind for her pastor whom she saw *in person* every week! Maybe a brand-new 747!

Shortly after that chance meeting with this lady, I was in my office when my secretary placed the annual giving records of our membership on my desk for my signature to make them official for the Internal Revenue Service.

My eye was caught by the top-giving record in the stack; it was this special lady's record.

I couldn't help but take a long, hard look at all the zeros that crossed the monthly record of her previous year's giving. This lady not only had failed to tithe to her church, but according to her record, she had not even given a simple dime, not any time, to any of the over 156 offerings that were taken in our church (which she had attended for the past year).

The next time I saw this lady, I stopped her and said, "Honey, help Brother John out a little bit. Can you tell me how you are going to give a Lear jet to the ministry you mentioned to me, when you have not given even one cent to your own local church?"

To my surprise, the lady was not daunted in the least by my question. She had her answer all ready. "Oh, Brother John, you don't understand — *when* we get rich, *when* we get a lot of wealth, *then* we are going to give the Lear jet, and *then* we'll also start giving huge amounts to the church. Brother John, please don't feel slighted, we'll even pay off the church mortgage!"

I shook my head at this poor, unfortunate, uninformed lady, and said, "Honey, you won't be able to give a dime to Ken Copeland or to your local church in the future. If you cannot give right now, the Word of God guarantees you won't be able to give anything to the Gospel when you get rich. Look up Luke 16:10 when you get home."

When that lady got home, if she took the time to look up Luke 16:10, she would have read the following:

> **He that is faithful in that which is least is faithful also in much: and he that is unjust in the least is unjust also in much.**

That poor lady and so many other Christians like her are doing it backwards! Their attitude is, "I cannot give when things are tight, but when I get plenty of money, I am going to give most of it to God." That is not what the Bible says.

If you have a heart for giving to God right now, and you want to assure yourself the privilege of giving to God all of the rest of your life, you had better start giving now!

Don't wait for riches! You see, if you can't give to God right now, where you currently are in your finances, whether that be a state of abundance or great shortage, you will not be able to *start* giving at some future date, even if a *billion* dollars somehow flows into your control.

Luke 16:10 says you must start giving right where you are. Faithfulness, when your money is in short supply, is a prerequisite to financial faithfulness when your money is in abundance.

We have already determined from Deuteronomy 8:18 that God has given you the supernatural power to get wealth, and that power is activated through your faithful giving to establish His covenant here on earth.

What is that covenant? Surely, since God has given us the awesome power to get wealth, we should know the precise nature of the covenant that our wealth-getting power was designed to establish.

So many Christians mistakenly think that this covenant is found in the first fourteen verses of Deuteronomy 28.

But that is not the covenant! You see, Deuteronomy 28:1-14 describes the blessings that the keepers of the covenant will receive from God.

This portion of Deuteronomy 28 says you will be blessed in the *city* and in the *field*, and in the *fruit of thy body*, and in thy *ground* and in thy *cattle*. It goes on and on for fourteen verses with the *blessings*. But that's not the covenant! These are the blessings that come to the person who *keeps* the covenant.

Let me now share the actual covenant with you. It is first spoken to Abram in its shortest form:

> Now the Lord had said unto Abram, Get thee out of thy country, and from thy kindred, and from thy father's house, unto a land that I will shew thee:
>
> And I will make of thee a great nation, and I will bless thee, and make thy name great; *and thou shalt be a blessing.*
>
> And I will bless them that bless thee, and curse him that curseth thee: and in thee shall all families of the earth be blessed.
>
> Genesis 12:1-3

Here's God's Covenant

Here are God's agreements:

1. **I will make of thee a great nation.**

2. **I will bless thee.**

3. **I will make thy name great.**

Here are the recipient's agreements:

1. Get out of the world system. Pry yourself away from your dependence upon your old economic base.

2. I will bless you — you will have a new economic base.

3. **Thou shalt be a blessing.** In thee **shall all the families of the earth be blessed.**

You see, a covenant cannot be a contract unless it involves commitment from both parties. Covenants are two-way agreements. Let me illustrate.

The joys in your marriage are the *blessings* of your marriage, but they are not the covenant. The covenant is to become one flesh and to face problems together in sickness and in health.

In God's covenant, the first three agreements are *His promises to you.* He will bless you with a seed (becoming a great nation). He will bless you (materially). He will bless you (through the powerful worldwide testimony of those who are the Sons of God). The Judeo-Christian name is the greatest name on earth.

Notice that at the beginning and at the end of the covenant God asks something in return. He tells you to:

1. Get out of the world's system.

2. Be a blessing.

God expects you to depend upon Him to bless you, and then to use those *blessings* to become a blessing to literally every human being in the earth.

Child of God, keep this in mind — *you cannot bless anybody unless you have first been blessed yourself.*

When you meet a hungry man, how are you going to feed him if you do not have more than enough food? The Apostle James said if you can't feed him, leave him alone. If you cannot give clothes to a naked man, get out of the way. Do not slobber all over someone in need of food and drink with empty prayers.

Give them what they need or do not give them anything at all. Those are harsh words but they are not *my* words, they are God's words. He says:

> **If a brother or sister be naked, and destitute of daily food,**
>
> **And one of you say unto them, Depart in peace, be ye warmed and filled; notwithstanding ye give them not those things which are needful to the body; what doth it profit?**
>
> **James 2:15,16**

Surely the Word of God does encourage the positive confession and every child of God should practice this scriptural exercise in overcoming evil. But you should *never* try to use a positive confession for others in need! We are commanded to meet their need with tangible goods out of the blessings that God promised to those who know how to receive from Him.

Do you see it? God blesses us and He expects us to be a blessing to others! Most of the Christians who are not receiving God's prosperity are not receiving it because they do not understand that the covenant of God promises blessings to us, so that we can *be a blessing.*

Simply stated, God gives us the *power* to get wealth to be a blessing to others. *Literally every lost person on the earth has the God-given right to expect something from every Christian he meets.* First and foremost, they have a right to expect the Gospel (good news) that a Savior has been born and is ready to save every one of them.

Church of God awaken! God is calling you to go *beyond your own personal blessings,* and *become a blessing!*

Now if this upsets you too much, *and you want to remain in poverty,* you sure can. There will always be room in this world for poor folks. God says so:

For the poor always ye have with you....
                                                    John 12:8a

There will always be someone around for the blessed to bless. But have you noticed that there is a shortage of people who are prepared (cash in pocket) to do the blessing?

Child of God, hear the Word.

There is a special group of people whom God will use through their obedience to His covenant, and these people will go forth with the God-given blessings of abundance and bless, bless, bless, bless everyone, everywhere they go.

They will faithfully operate the power to get wealth given to them by God. They will do this by consistently planting their tithes and offerings, in the good ground of Christ-honoring churches and ministries. They will, through the faithful operation of God's clearly stated law of increase, be a blessing to others, even as God promised in His Word they would be.

Child of God, the covenant is already working in the lives of many of God's sons and daughters. I assure you on the authority of God's Word *it can and it will work in your life also.*

Be assured, as you seek first the Kingdom of God and His righteousness, all these things that you desire will be added to you. (Matt. 6:33.)

4
Patience —
The Missing Ingredient

Contrary to popular teachings, if you want to experience God's abundance in your life, being a blessing to others everywhere, you must understand *it is not enough to just have "faith."*

Remember the fellow I told you about driving "Old PRAYED 4?" Faith alone did not unlock God's treasure chest of abundance in his life. Here is the key ingredient that must accompany faith for you to be able to receive from God.

That ye be not slothful, but followers of them who through faith *and patience* inherit the promises.
Hebrews 6:12

You see, you inherit God's promises through faith *and* through patience. If you want to experience the blessings of reaping, you must first sow seeds in faith. Then, only after patience has done its perfect work will you begin to reap that which you sowed.

There is a season of *planting* (sowing), and there is a season of *growing* (patience), and then there is a season of *harvesting* (reaping). Let me give a personal illustration.

In November of 1985, my wife, Pat and I, planted the biggest seed that we have ever planted in our lives. As I look back on it, I can hardly believe the size of the seed. We planted it in obedience to God, *before* God even told us what the seed was for.

In the past, we used to plant seed for specific projects. This time, however, God told us to plant in faith and patiently wait until *later* when He would show us what we were planting for.

After a few months of patiently waiting, as my wife and I were driving to a special ministry service in our car, God's presence just seemed to fill the entire car. All of a sudden, God revealed to us the next step in our ministry. He laid out a plan that would allow us to encircle the globe with the message of God's abundance.

We had been praying for that. We had been patiently waiting for His direction. Our divine direction was unfolding, and my wife and I now realized *we had already planted the seed for the much needed finances for this new adventure.*

Praise God! We serve an abundant God, the God of the harvest. Give *Him* the Glory! Remember, *sowing* (faith), *growing* (patience), *then reaping* (realization)!

The Living Bible says it clearly in 2 Corinthians 9:6-7a and 10:

> But remember this — if you give little, you will get little. A farmer who plants just a few seeds will get only a small crop, but if he plants much, he will reap much.
>
> Every one must make up his own mind as to how much he should give.
>
> For God, who gives seed to the farmer to plant, and *later on,* good crops to harvest and eat, will give

you more and more seed to plant and will make it grow so that you can give away more and more fruit from your harvest.

And in Galatians, we are reminded:

> Be not deceived; God is not mocked: for whatsoever a man soweth, that shall he also reap.
> **Galatians 6:7**

From these two Scriptures, it becomes clear that we *never* reap in the same season that we sow. There is a definite *time* between the seeding and the harvest — a time of *patiently waiting* for the planted seed to grow into the desired harvest.

Child of God, open your eyes and realize that through the laws of the harvest — sowing, growing, *then* reaping — God has given you the *power* to get great wealth so that His covenant may be established.

Now let me be quick to say that along with all of God's ordained ministries, God's covenant is *not just* for Christian television and more evangelistic crusades. His covenant is also for local churches, blessing every family in their community in every way that they need help.

The message of Jesus will come to the world partly through television and partly through world evangelization, but still, first and foremost, there must be a strong local church in every neighborhood of every city throughout the entire world.

Just as the TV ministries and evangelistic campaigns need money, so too churches need money. It takes money to build the buildings, to provide the heat, and to teach the *principles* of the Kingdom of God to every creature in every community.

Never underestimate the importance of the following verse of Scripture. No matter what your endtime theology may be, *all* endtime theology agrees on this one point — that we must bring the message of the Kingdom of God to everyone on planet earth as fast as we can to see the King of kings and Lord of lords return.

> And this *gospel of the kingdom* shall be preached in all the world for a witness unto all nations; *and then* shall the end come.
>
> **Matthew 24:14**

Another thing that *all* endtime theology agrees upon is that the taking of the Gospel of the Kingdom of God to the world will take vast sums of money.

Friend, hear me on this. Sacrificial giving (although God many times leads us to give sacrificially) will not bring our King back. The scope of financing this great worldwide project of evangelization that God has now begun in these last days cannot be accomplished by sacrificial giving alone. This endtime harvest of the earth will take almost *all* the wealth of the earth to accomplish.

And where is most of the earth's wealth today?

It is an established fact that the saints surely do not have it. It does not take a genius to know where the world's wealth is today. The wicked of the world have it. How many Christians do you know who have vast amounts of money?

Yet, for the Kingdom of God to be established, for the churches to be built, for world global Christian TV to be established, for much-needed preachers to be trained, for evangelists to go — it will take more money than the church and its members now control.

Most Christians do not have the vaguest idea of how much wealth there is in our world today. Just look at this.

I know one purchasing agent for a rich oil sheik. He tells me that when this sheik wants a McDonald's hamburger feast, he will put his entire family and crew into his 747, and off they will fly to the nearest country with a McDonald's restaurant. It might cost $20,000 for one night at McDonald's!

When this same sheik sends his wives to London to shop, he puts them in his private jet — a flying palace if you please — and burns up $17,500 just for fuel. Then, his wives have been known to spend a million dollars in the morning, and two million dollars in the afternoon on jewels, furs, shoes, furniture, cars, and other things (wines, foods, antiques, and so on).

That's just the wealth of one man!

For you to grasp the significance of how much wealth there really is in this world, I have written the following two chapters to help you to destroy *your own limited perceptions* of just how important wealth is, and how much wealth there really is in this rich world God created. These chapters will put to rest once and for all the devil's doctrine that there's not enough.

5

Why Christians Should Control the World's Wealth

For *I was envious* at the foolish, when I saw *the prosperity of the wicked.*

Psalm 73:3

Until I went into the sanctuary of God; *then* understood I their end.

Psalm 73:17

...And *the wealth of the sinner is* laid up for the just.

Proverbs 13:22b

Child of God, for us to begin to get even a vague notion of the enormous effects the wealth of the wicked will have upon the Church of God, and the rapid evangelization of the world in these last days, you must first begin to understand, in very general, rounded numbers just how much wealth there really is in the world!

I honestly believe most Christians do not even remotely realize the amazing amount of material wealth our great God of abundance has deposited here when He created this marvelous, opulent planet.

Before you can appreciate how much wealth God has placed in this world, it is *first* necessary for you to understand *why* it is important for Christians to have control of that wealth.

In fact, most of the Christians I know have a hard time visualizing anything more than the meager amounts of money they personally have control of as the direct result of their weekly paychecks. What they mistakingly call the good life consists of a car or two in their garage, several rooms of furniture, and perhaps a modest home they are in the process of buying back from the bank.

That is it. That is the extent of the average Christian's knowledge of the "good life."

I have heard hundreds upon hundreds of good-hearted, sincere Christians tell me, "Brother John, I've got all I need, I'm blessed. I'm blessed. I'm blessed. I just don't need anymore."

Well, maybe *you do* have all of your needs met. Maybe *you are* blessed with everything you need to achieve an acceptable standard of living, but what about the wretched state of those billions of lost souls on our planet? They may have material possessions, but no one has told them about the King of kings, and about His marvelous Kingdom principles that will set them free!

What about the ineffective, crippled condition of the Body of Christ, often unable to move forward *in power* because they do not have the proper funds necessary?

Imagine with me for a moment. If you were bombarded by wealth, if you had literally hundreds of thousands of dollars more than you personally needed come into your control to do with as you wished, surely you, as a child of God, would give the greater part of that excess wealth to the things of God. What better use could you find for your money? What better way to invest your funds than in God's final, endtime harvest, bringing billions of lost souls to salvation?

The attitude that so many Christians possess today to strive and struggle just to simply "have enough" is not a scriptural motivation, and it is totally out of step with the great commission given us by our Lord Jesus.

It is actually a selfish motivation! The "I've got enough" kind of thinking is an evil seed sown in our mind by the enemy of the Gospel, the devil himself.

Here is God's plan for your finances:

> **And God is able to make all grace abound toward you; (why?) that ye, always having all sufficiency in all things, may abound to every good work** [being the blessing God wants you to be].
>
> **2 Corinthians 9:8**

The Church of God cannot properly grow, it cannot minister through the marvelous medium of television, it cannot minister through global satellite hookups, it cannot minister in much-needed literature, it cannot minister through millions upon millions of debt-free churches, bombarding the earth with the Gospel of the Kingdom of God *until* it produces a breed of saints who are not satisfied with just enough, but who recognize that their God has called them to financial blessings that will bring forth *abundantly more than enough!*

Only then can they give the significant amounts needed to the churches, television ministries, evangelists, teachers, apostles, and prophets to reach the whole world.

Only then can they give the significant amounts needed to buy satellite time to shower the world in a total, twenty-four-hour-a-day Christian blitz that He (Jesus) is the King of kings and Lord of lords.

Recently I participated in a Christian telethon where one wealthy lady phoned in and pledged $750,000 in one donation! Another person called and gave $500,000! There were also thousands of pledges of smaller amounts that enabled this Christian TV network to operate for a few months in a few cities.

Just imagine for a moment if *all* of these thousands of small donors had the money that those two rich saints had! Don't you know that they would have gladly given as much as the two rich saints did? Can you imagine just how quickly that one TV network could fill the world with the Gospel of Jesus Christ if all the saints who donated had abundant giving potential?

Now don't get me wrong on this. I am not espousing a theology of giving that places undue importance upon wealthy people. After all, Jesus always looked at the heart of the giver, *not* the amount given.

Remember, in the eyes of Jesus, the widow who gave the two mites outgave everyone else in the temple, because she gave out of bare necessity, not luxury.

In these endtimes, I do believe God is raising a special people to receive abundant wealth — a peculiar people who will be willing and soon able to give large portions of wealth, a people who will take the Bible literally in one of the most amazing transfers of wealth ever envisioned. They will be a people of faith in the literal interpretation of God's Word.

They will finance the great endtime harvest of God.

When God has a *plan*, He always *empowers his people* to accomplish His plan. Jesus always did what was needed to feed His people, and to provide them with the necessary tools that they needed to preach the Gospel.

He told the apostles where to cast their nets for the greatest catch of fish. He told Peter how to get a coin from the mouth of a fish.

Nothing is different today, except the super expense of the necessary technology needed to bring the full Gospel to the world. In these last days, God knows that preaching the Gospel is not inexpensive.

For example, to allow a Christian broadcasting network to broadcast from a communication satellite for just one month, the cost is about $250,000 in satellite rental fees and related costs! A simple television camera to film a Christian television production can easily cost $85,000, and usually a minimum of three cameras are involved.

The production studio that films these Christian programs requires video tape recorders that cost another $250,000 each. And to do the job properly, the television production people tell me they need about four of these recorders.

That is not all! At just one television station, there are sometimes five or six studios, and each studio has to be equipped with the same cameras, the same video equipment, and the same amount of production people to make these programs happen. Keep in mind that there are also the ongoing labor costs for the operation of all of these pieces of equipment, along with any travel, lodging, and food for guests.

Please notice, I have not begun to mention all the buildings, towers for antennas, and other support structures!

Child of God, I am told by experts that to properly put a Christian television station on the air costs as much as ten million dollars!

Oh sure, there are some Christian television stations currently operating in North America that are working from much smaller budgets, but let's be brutally frank. These low-budget Christian stations are barely on the air. They are pressed from crisis telethon to crisis telethon, trying to stay just one jump ahead of losing their signal because of a severe shortage of equipment, manpower and money. Now, how many heathens will stay tuned to a channel that is constantly pressing for much needed funds?

Now I know that's a strong statement, but put yourself in the heathen's mind for a moment. Honestly, wouldn't you just click your dial right past these low-budget Christian television shows when you see a fuzzy picture of some people sitting around a very plain set, and every other week pressing for funds in a crisis telethon?

As a heathen, why should you watch this type of show when you can turn to an expensively produced, well-funded program on a secular channel?

This is *not an indictment* of low-budget Christian television! The fact is, if sufficient money were in the hands of the smaller station owners, they would and could produce the same high-quality productions as the world does but with a much more wholesome context.

I know that they are doing the best they can with the money you and other Christians are currently giving them! Unfortunately, too many Christian television stations simply do not have the proper funds. So in the eyes of the unsaved, these Christian stations and programs appear to lag behind the secular stations in eye appeal and broadcast quality.

Child of God, that is why reproducing another generation of Christians who are just "blessed," but not adequately blessed to pass a good portion of that blessing on for the evangelization of the world, is not meeting the needs of this last hour.

Each month, often without cost for my time, I work with many Christian television stations and networks in this land, helping them raise the much-needed support by teaching their viewers the promises and blessings of giving. Why?

Because there are billions of souls who need to be reached! We need a *new mentality of abundance,* an endtime generation of saints with an eye open to God's endtime takeover of this world's wealth.

Do you see where I am heading with this very practical, nuts-and-bolts revelation? Having enough for *yourself* is *not having enough!* You need enough for you *and* enough to give generously to fund every minister

God directs you to support, so that the Gospel can be quickly brought to others.

The wealth I am speaking of here is not just for another luxury car *it is for another soul!*

6
How Much Wealth
Is in the World?

Now, in the interest of more souls, let us take a look at this mind-expanding question: *just how much wealth is there in this world?*

After even a few simple calculations, the answer to this question will absolutely amaze and shock you! From this mind-expanding information, you can increase your expectation of the money God can put into your hands.

First, let's look at the value of some of the more common minerals on the face of God's earth. At today's rate of production, and at today's values (not allowing at all for future inflation), here are the approximate dollar values of just some of our major minerals which will be produced in the next twenty years:

- 220 billion dollars of copper
- 50 trillion dollars of gold
- 300 billion dollars of silver
- 360 billion dollars of aluminum
- 600 billion dollars of iron, tin, zinc, and lead

Keep this in mind, this is all *new wealth!*

In these eight minerals alone, in the next twenty years, we will produce *fifty-one trillion, four hundred and eighty billion* dollars worth of new wealth!

Other common items that will be produced in that same twenty years will be:

- 16 trillion dollars of oil

- 1.5 trillion dollars of barley

- 4 trillion dollars of corn

- 19 trillion dollars of meat

- 4 trillion dollars of rice

- 4 trillion dollars of pork

- 3.6 trillion dollars of wheat

Again, just in these few substances, you already are looking at another *fifty-two trillion, one hundred million dollars of new wealth!*

Today, by very conservative estimates, worldwide coal reserves alone are figured at about *three hundred and eighty-three trillion dollars* of wealth sitting on or just beneath our earth's crust!

Are you beginning to understand how much abundant wealth God has created? He has deposited *more then enough* fuel on this planet to take care of all our energy needs, present and future.

Just from these few minerals, crops, herds, and our known coal reserves, in twenty years, we are seeing a world wealth increase of about *four hundred and eighty-six trillion, five hundred and eighty million dollars.*

In the electric energy field alone, the estimated kilowatt hours of reserves (not counting coal) are another *six hundred trillion dollars!*

Child of God, just in the items I've listed so far, we are already more than 1,086 trillion dollars in wealth, and we are just beginning!

There is such an abundance of simple mineral and material wealth in this world that in just one category, explosives, man today has already created 28,000 pounds (TNT equivalent) of explosives for every man, woman, and child on the face of this earth! That is fourteen tons of explosives per person already created!

That surely should be more than enough. Yet, when you complete this chapter, you will come to understand that the raw materials of this world are so abundant that there are *tons* of almost every type of material for every man, woman, boy and girl on planet earth.

In the United States alone, one reliable source estimated that 88 percent of all the money legally circulated by the United States Mint is currently unaccounted for!

Federal economists speculate that there is so much currency available, such an abundance, that a good percentage of the cash is the readily available, "on-hand" cash kept in people's pockets, or hidden away in private stashes, under beds, in walls, or buried in backyards.

Some of the money is probably overseas, and much of it is in the underworld (in the possession of criminals and drug kingpins — the wicked of our society).

Whatever the speculation, *134 billion dollars* in U.S. currency is now currently unaccounted for! *And,* amazing as it may seem, there are more one-hundred dollar bills in circulation than one dollar bills — as much as sixty times more!

No wonder Christians have so much trouble getting their hands on money — they are going after the one dollar bills, and there's a shortage of them! They need to start going after the one-hundred dollar bills — there's sixty times more of them!

The January 13, 1986, issue of *U.S. News and World Report* says that there is one millionaire in every *one hundred* households in the United States!

To give you an idea of how unevenly that wealth is currently distributed, *U.S. News and World Report* also reveals some rather shocking facts. Although U.S. millionaires make up only 1 percent of the American population:

• They hold one-third of the nation's private wealth.

• They own 60 percent of the nation's corporate stocks.

• They possess 30 percent of all interest-bearing assets.

• They own 9 percent of all the country's real estate.

• About 80 percent of all millionaires come from middle — or working-class families. Think about this — our millionaires are being produced, not from the rich class, but from the poor and middle class!

Why am I writing about these things in a Christian book? Because you need to know that wealth is not some distant, impossible thing, but is a real possibility for *you*.

You need to understand that wealth is not as scarce as you are often led to believe. Once you begin to grasp that reality, then God can begin to direct that available wealth into your hands.

In the next twenty years, it is conservatively estimated that there will be 35,120,000 housing starts, with an average price of $95,000 per unit. That's *three trillion, three hundred and thirty-six million billion, four hundred million* in new homes — just in the U.S. — just in the next twenty years!

To begin to estimate the total wealth, the total value of current, existing real estate in the world would take far more of a research budget than this book allows.

Some rather simple deductions can be made.

If there were only one house for every ten people in the world, that would mean there are 450 million residences in the world. *If* each residence had an average, extremely conservative value of only $40,000, then the personal dwelling of the world alone would equal another $18 *trillion!*

Naturally, these conservative figures do not even count commercial real estate, which is well over $100 trillion.

Remember how a few years ago everyone was saying that the world population was exploding, and that in a few years there would not be any room left for anyone? Despite all the gloom and doom of the population explosion movements, the simple truth is: *The physical resources of earth can now support all of our multiplying humanity at higher standards of living than anyone has ever experienced in the history of man!*

Child of God, I believe that statement is so vital, so critical to your understanding of God's multiplying abundance, that I want to repeat it: *The physical resources of earth can now support all of our multiplying humanity at higher standards of living than anyone has ever experienced in the history of man!*

One study showed that if we could gather the entire population of the world together, and have them stand up, without touching anyone else, allowing a space 2.6 square feet for each person, that the entire population of the world could easily fit into the city limits of Jacksonville, Florida, with plenty of room to spare![1]

Here is how the numbers break down:

The city limits of Jacksonville, Florida, contain 841 square miles. Each square mile contains 27,878,400 square feet. The total number of square feet in the city is 23,445,734,000. The world population is approximately four and a half billion people. So, by allowing an average of 2.6 square feet for each person from babies to adults, every person in the world could stand shoulder to shoulder *in just one-half of the city limits of the city of Jacksonville, Florida!*

Do you honestly think for one minute that God would allow billions of people on this earth, and not

---

[1]Robert L. Sassone, *Handbook on Population*, 3rd ed., formerly published as *Report to California Legislature on Population at the Request of the Office of the Senate Majority Leader*, 1973. p. 94.

give them enough room to live? Of course not. And the earth's ability to absorb the population of man is only getting better.

Yes, I am aware that there are famines in Ethiopia and other parts of Africa, and around the world people are dying of starvation.

When you investigate these famines, you will come to understand that they are not the result of God's earth failing to produce adequate food, they are the direct result of man failing to adequately distribute the food that is being produced!

For example, India does not have a famine problem because of a lack of food; it has a hunger problem because of religious beliefs which are contrary to the Word of God.

The Hindu religion teaches that people who die are then reincarnated as animals. As such, all animals in India become sacred, and then cannot be killed. It is against the law to kill rats, mice, cows, etc. That deception of Satan is what causes the severe food shortage in India.

You see, every cow in India eats enough food to feed seven people, and there are about two hundred million "sacred" cows in India!

If India would just stop feeding these cows, they would have enough grain to feed *one billion, four hundred million people!* India would actually become a food exporting nation if we could just get them evangelized!

You see, God has provided the food. It is only man's own folly caused by his ignorance of God's Word that has caused the famines. India has enough food to feed one-fourth of the entire world's population!

As staggering as the *raw material wealth* in the world is, there is yet another form of wealth that has already begun to transfer to the Christian community. That is the accumulated sum of what men have learned, a knowledge concentrated in machines and processes. For example, when you pick up a simple ball point pen, although it has only ten or fifteen cents worth of *raw material wealth* in it, literally millions of dollars of technology has gone into developing that first ball point pen.

That *accumulated wealth* is then passed on to anyone who has the small change it takes to buy a ball point pen in the local department store. The simple ball point pen is a form of wealth that benefits from men's ability to do in concert what they cannot do by themselves.

When the simple, *raw material* wealth that we have barely covered here — totaling well over *one thousand trillion dollars* — is then multiplied by *the accumulated wealth* of processing, it is easy to see that the world has literally *millions* of *trillions* of dollars — enough for every man, woman, and child on the planet to be a millionaire many times over!

But wealth is more than materials; wealth is also an enhancement of access. Today it takes man five hours to cross a continent, not the three days it used to take by car, or the three months it used to take by covered wagon.

The tires on your car now run 40,000 miles, not 8,000. These inventions give man increased time, the most valuable form of *all* wealth!

Satellites now enable the Body of Christ to reach millions of people at the same time. This technology that *multiplies* time is now primarily in the hands of the wicked, but God is rapidly putting that technology in the hands of the just!

God will logarithmically increase our ability to reach many. The technology that created those satellites, launched them into space, and then allowed us access to them is a form of wealth that did not even exist twenty years ago!

Let us look at another example. We talked earlier about the *raw material* wealth of oil reserves. This *raw material* wealth actually increases when the oil is processed into gasoline.

Look at the *time* Mother Nature has invested in creating these oil reserves. Nature has invested millions of dollars in every gallon of petroleum we harvest!

Man's wealth is also his heritage of the time invested and the time we inherit from others. Controlled time is probably the greatest wealth of all.

The harnessed energy, production, distribution, communication tools, and techno-scientific literacy we inherit *all* combine to produce prosperity and wealth.

You see, the *wealth of the wicked*, for a great part, is already in our hands.

Computer technology is in our hands. Satellite technology is in our hands. This vital endtime prophecy of the wealth of the wicked being laid up for the just is already in the process of being fulfilled!

Finally, there's another *key spiritual principle* you need to understand about wealth: Real wealth cannot be used to alter yesterday. Real wealth can only be used to alter today and tomorrow. And, the more wealth is employed, the more it is multiplied.

For example, the *raw material* in a satellite might amount to a few thousand dollars. But when those raw materials are formed and shaped by man, when they benefit from the combined energies of man and processes already created by others, *then* the *refined wealth* of that satellite is in the hundreds of millions of dollars!

You see, the wealth has actually increased! Gold, silver, copper, oil, and so on, have no real value until they serve some defined monetary or technological function for man.

For example, gold is precious because it is scarce, and because the nations of the world have agreed it should become one of their main forms of monetary exchange.

Silver's value comes primarily from the various technological uses it has in commercial industries. As new technological uses are found for the various minerals on our earth, the value of these minerals goes up, thus actually increasing the wealth we have in our world!

With each new invention that increases man's potential to produce more energy, we have *more wealth*, not less.

When men of science learn how to change sea water into fuel for engines (don't laugh, sea water is hydrogen and oxygen, both highly volatile elements), the whole of the seven seas will become worth more than our current computer capacity can calculate.

As much as our wealth is increasing, or will increase, our time is not an unlimited commodity. That is why we must reach the lost souls of the world, now.

Remember Revelation 10:6 says there will come a moment when there will be no more time:

> **And sware by him that liveth for ever and ever, who created heaven, and the things that therein are, and the earth, and the things that therein are, and the sea, and the things which are therein, that *there should be time no longer.***

What we do to reach the world, we must do now, and God has provided us with all we need.

The wealth *and* the technology needed to reach this world with the Gospel is available right now!

Christians must learn that God does intend for them to have the wealth of the wicked — so they can use it to finance God's endtime harvest!

7

God Wants You To Have Wealth

There is one very definite thing we do know about the nature of our God. He is:

> ...the same yesterday, and to day, and for ever.
> **Hebrews 13:8**

If, as I have shown from Scripture, *the wealth of the wicked is laid up for the just, then* it stands to reason that this endtime people of God who are alive today will be the witnesses of the outpouring of this financial abundance. They will surely be the ones to see this great, endtime transfer of the wealth of the wicked right into the hands of God's properly prepared people.

I am talking about *literally more than enough* wealth to establish a worldwide Kingdom that will never end; a Kingdom that will alleviate every need known to mankind: spiritual, physical, and yes, even financial.

Now child of God, I understand that for this endtime prophecy to be worthy of your consideration, one of the key tests it must pass is that it *must be consistent with God's word, and with the very nature of God,* which is the same yesterday, today, and forever!

In this chapter and the next one, I will soundly establish from Scripture that this endtime transfer of the finances of the wicked to the children of God *really is* part of His divine plan.

God Previously Has Given the Wealth of the Wicked to His Children

The best way I know to establish this truth is by proving from Scripture, that God throughout history has given the wealth of the wicked to His children on a consistent basis.

To determine the clear Biblical answer to this question, "Is it within God's pre-determined plan to periodically hand over the wealth of the wicked to the just?" let me begin this study of God's Word by drawing your attention to Proverbs 13:22:

> **A good man leaveth an inheritance to his children's children: and the wealth of the sinner [wicked] is laid up for the just.**
>
> **Proverbs 13:22**

This passage is obviously talking about actual, *real* wealth. Hard assets, if you please. God intends for every good man (person) to leave an inheritance for his children, *and* his grandchildren!

Observe what you just read. If the first half of this verse is correct, then surely it disproves the old notion that God wants His children to be poor and barely able to get by. How can a poor man who was barely able to get by from day to day leave any financial inheritance to his children?

But let us get back to the second half of this verse, and hear where this wealth is to come from.

Child of God, our great God is currently allowing the sinners to stack up great sums of wealth for the just (the sons and daughters of God). This two-part Scripture obviously deals with the money of the wicked, and God's plans for the transfer of that monetary wealth to the justified ones. God plainly states that the precious possessions of the wealthy wicked are waiting for transfer to the account of the just (justified).

In another portion of Scripture, God again speaks of literally stripping the wealth of cheats, racketeers, loan sharks, and even so-called legitimate lending establishments that gouge their customers with unreasonable interest rates and hidden loan costs, and giving that ill-gotten wealth to those who will pity the poor.

> **He that by usury and unjust gain increaseth his substance, he shall gather it for him that will pity the poor.**
>
> **Proverbs 28:8**

Do you see it? The Bible says that all of the money that the wicked are gathering through unjust methods (cheating, racketeering, loan sharking, etc.), will have to eventually be given up to those who will "pity the poor." This verse clearly says that the wicked are gathering it for those who will pity the poor.

Now I ask you, "Who will pity the poor?" Certainly not the unjust or the wicked. I'll tell you who will pity the poor — it is the true Christian church! It is for you and me that God has these unsuspecting, evil men gathering money so that we can, in accordance with God's commands, meet the needs of the poor. (James 2:15-16.)

And here's the good part. When we do control this wealth and we faithfully distribute it to meet the needs of the poor and hungry of this world, then *God will give it right back to us!*

> **He that hath pity upon the poor lendeth unto the Lord, and** *that which he hath given will he pay him again.*
>
> **Proverbs 19:17**

Isn't that a wonderful plan? When we faithfully fulfill the financial plan of God, we set up a perpetual cycle of wealth that circulates finances from the wicked to the saints of God to the needs of this world, and then back into the hands of the faithful! Praise God!

Now I want you to read one of the most amazing Scriptures in the entire Bible:

> **For God giveth to a man that is good in his sight wisdom, and knowledge, and joy:** *but to the sinner he giveth travail, to gather and to heap up, that he may give to him that is good before God.*
>
> **Ecclesiastes 2:26a**

Do you see what I am seeing? God has a ministry for every lost man and woman. If that sounds like bad theology, look at this verse again. God has every lost person out there gathering up and heaping up wealth. God's Word literally says that He gives to them the task of gathering up and heaping up wealth for those who are good before God.

Can you imagine how great the "travail" of these sinners will be as God starts this miraculous prophetic transfer of their wealth into the hands of those who are good before God?

Who are these people who are called good before God? According to the Word of God, the only people anywhere referred to as "good before God" are the precious people who have been washed in the blood of the Lamb. Saved folks, born-again folks like you and me!

Child of God, surely you are starting to see the overall magnitude of this great revelation. Notice, *this is not some isolated verse or two that we base our conclusions on.* But, the Word of God abounds with scriptural references to the fact that the wealth of the wicked is laid up for the just.

Look at several more verses.

> **There is an evil** [a distressing thing] **which I have seen under the sun, and it is common among men** [it happens all the time]:
>
> **A man to whom God hath given riches, wealth, and honour, so that he wanteth nothing for his soul of all that he desireth, yet** *God giveth him not power to eat thereof, but a stranger eateth it.*
>
> **Ecclesiastes 6:1,2a**

This Scripture boldly declares that *it is common among men* that God will allow one man to gather great sums of riches and wealth, but that the man who gathered it will not have the "power" (ability) to eat from that which he has gathered.

Instead, a virtual stranger will enjoy all the wealth that the rich man has gathered and heaped up.

This passage speaks of a stranger eating that wealth, and who is more of a "stranger" to a wealthy, wicked man than a Godly, moral, well-informed Christian?

The world's wicked rich are unwittingly involved in a futile operation. They are busy, day and night, nonstop, gathering and heaping up so that they can give all the wealth they gather to total strangers (the sons and daughters of God)!

Read further. In Isaiah, the entire 61st chapter deals with God's abundance flowing into the hands of God's people. Read it. It is in your Bible!

> **And strangers shall stand and feed your flocks, and the sons of the alien shall be your plowmen and your vinedressers.**
>
> **But ye shall be named the Priests of the Lord: men shall call you the Ministers of our God: ye shall eat the riches of the Gentiles, and in their glory shall ye boast yourselves.**
>
> **Isaiah 61:5,6**

Notice that in Ecclesiastes 6:1,2, it says that strangers will eat the wealth of the rich. Compare that with Isaiah 61:5,6, which declares you shall eat the riches of the nations. Contrary to popular teaching and tradition, God does *not intend* for the righteous to be hopeless slaves to the spirit of poverty!

Once again, read how great an abundance He intends for the righteous to stack up:

> **If thou return to the Almighty, thou shalt be built up, thou shalt put away iniquity far from thy tabernacles.**
>
> **Then shalt thou lay up gold as dust, and the *gold of O'phir as the stones of the brooks.***
>
> *Yea, the Almighty shall be thy defence, and thou shalt have plenty of silver.*
>
> **Job 22:23-25**

According to this passage, as you separate yourself from unrighteousness and turn yourself more to God and righteous living, God intends for you to have gold as abundantly "as the stones" in a brook.

This same verse also says God intends for you to have "plenty of silver." You see, the very nature of God is abundance not poverty. Surely this speaks of more than "just enough," or barely making it.

Our God is without a doubt the God of abundance! Remember, He said:

> **I am come that they** [you and I] **might have life, and that they** [meaning us] **might have it** *more abundantly.*
>
> **John 10:10b**

Perhaps the clearest passage anywhere in the Bible that declares God's intention to give the Godly the wealth of the wicked sinners of this world appears in Job 27:13-17. Please hear it with open ears:

> **This is the portion of a wicked man with God, and the heritage of oppressors, which they shall receive of the Almighty.**
>
> **If his children be multiplied, it is for the sword: and his offspring shall not be satisfied with bread.**
>
> **These that remain of him shall be buried in death: and his widows shall not weep.**
>
> **Though he heap up silver as the dust, and prepare raiment as the clay;**
>
> **He may prepare it, but the just shall put it on, and the innocent shall divide the silver.**
>
> **Job 27:13-17**

You see, the wicked man's ultimate portion with God is not very abundant. His children will be slaughtered. His offspring shall not be satisfied. He shall be buried, unsaved, and his widow will not even cry.

Though he heaps up fine garments in abundance, and silver like dust, "the innocent," bloodwashed Christians shall put on those expensive garments and *they shall divide the silver of the wicked men amongst themselves.*

God's clearly stated intention is to loot the wicked, and give their wealth to the just. This is clearly stated in these and many other verses of Scripture. When I say that many other verses speak of this ongoing transfer of wealth from the wicked to the just, I am not just speaking off the top of my head. There are simply too many of them to list here at this time.

Surely these I have listed are enough to unquestionably establish this truth. Remember:

> **In the mouth of two or three witnesses shall every word be established.**
>
> **2 Corinthians 13:1b**

Many more than two or three Scripture witnesses have been given to substantiate this truth from God's Word. Surely these establish that "the wealth of the wicked is laid up for the just."

David the psalmist's attention once was drawn to the enormous wealth of the wicked, and he was very troubled, even envious, when he saw that the wicked possessed the greater part of the earth's wealth. But when he went into the sanctuary of God, where he found God's mind on the matter, David came to understand that evil men's final days were controlled by God.

> **For I was envious...when I saw the *prosperity of the wicked*.**
>
> **Psalm 73:3**

> **Until I went into the sanctuary of God; *then* understood I their end.**
>
> **Psalm 73:17**

Yes, the wicked are prospering now.

Yes, it would be easy to be envious of their unbelievable wealth. Recently, a deposed ex-president of an Asian country was driven from office. News reports on reputable television stations reported the worth of this *one man* to be over thirty billion dollars!

Child of God, do you have any idea how much 30 billion dollars is? Let me try to illustrate it in a way that our minds can grasp.

If you lived in a city with a population of 100,000 people, 30 billion dollars would be enough money to give every family in that city approximately $300,000! That is almost a third of a million dollars each. Isn't that staggering that the wealth of only one man could be so great?

Child of God, this is not a rare exception; there are many men in the earth today with this amount of wealth.

When you go into God's Word, when you seek His mind through the Scriptures, as we have done in this chapter, you will come to a new understanding of the end of the wealthy wicked.

You see, it is obvious from Scripture that *the wealth of the wicked is laid up for the just!*

Please do not misunderstand what I am saying here. Of course, spiritual matters *do* come first. But, child of God, hear me carefully. There exists a very dangerous, false attitude among Christians in our land today that absolutely is not supported by the Bible.

Many Christians are in great peril by functioning under the misconception that somehow being poor is a Godly thing.

You have probably met or know of some mistaken saints who have fallen prey to this deceptive lie of the devil. You can probably even tell me about some of these precious, well-meaning people you have met. You may have even given them a "love gift" at one time or another, or brought over a basket of food for their family.

These misinformed Christians are very serious about their spirituality. But, do their beliefs line up with the Scriptures you have just read? I say they do not!

Scripture says a good man should leave a financial inheritance for his children and grandchildren. (Proverbs 13:22.) What kind of a financial inheritance can these poverty-praising people leave?

When these people die, their spouses and children will testify that they were "good persons," but what does the Word of God say about them? God's Holy Word says that good men (men and women) leave an inheritance, even to their grandchildren!

Child of God, hear me loud and clear on this: Abject poverty, ignorance, and starvation are *not* God's perfect will for His children. He did not create a world of lack. He did not envision a Kingdom of want; He created a world of abundance! The poverty and insufficiency that we now witness in the world are the creation of the evil one: want, hunger, disease, and death are the best that his depraved nature could bring forth.

Now, please, please do not go off and quote me wrong on this. I *did not say* that any Christian who is poor is not a good person.

I *did not say* that being poor is a sure sign that a person is not spiritual.

What I am saying is that being poor is *not a Biblical sign* that a person *is* spiritual! Poverty actually contradicts what God's Word says about being a good man. (Prov. 13:22.)

Of course, leaving a financial inheritance is not *all* that God's Word says about being a good man, but it is definitely *one element* of the legacy of a good man. So why leave this part of the message off when discussing what God expects for and from good men and women?

As God's Word will clearly show us in the next chapter, being wealthy does *not* make a person a sinner.

Child of God, before you start listening to what Satan is saying in your ear, as he tries to tell you that all of my quotations concerning wealth and caring are being quoted from the Old Testament, remember that this concept of providing financially for our children is also re-emphasized strongly in your New Testament:

> **But if any provide not for his own, and specially for those of his own house, he hath denied the faith, and is *worse than an infidel*.**
>
> **1 Timothy 5:8**

Those are not my words, they are *God's* words! But, try as you may, you won't hear 1 Timothy 5:8 quoted in this welfare ridden society, much less from the conventional timid church pulpits where the emphasis is upon meeting the church budget instead of meeting the people's needs.

Why don't we hear more of this? Because it is too strong, too harsh for most of the "pie in the sky in the sweet bye and bye club" Christians to receive.

God is not timid or quiet about His opinion. He clearly states that He *does* expect you to provide for your wife, for your children, and even your children's children.

Friend, if you want to argue about these principles of Biblical economics, debate them with God, not Brother John. For these are clearly *His* principles; these are *His* desires for *His* people! These concepts are precise quotations from *His* own Holy Word.

Strange as it may seem, many will ignorantly continue to argue, "Brother John, you don't know the facts. Jesus was very poor and lived in abject poverty, without any earthly possessions. And since *He* is our main example of how Christians should live, I believe that if Jesus saw no value in the things of this earth, then we should see no value in such things either."

As I stated at the beginning of this chapter, the nature of God must be the same yesterday, today, and forever. I do believe a careful study of God's Word will show you that there are many signs and indicators that Jesus was *not* a poor man, but rather, a man with all the substance He needed to operate His ministry effectively in the culture and economy of His day.

Never once do you find anywhere in Scripture that Jesus had to utter the cry of today's church, with its apparent ignorance of the true Biblical principles of economics. Can you ever imagine Jesus saying: "The

Father is leading me to care for these twenty orphan children, but I won't be able to do it because I do not have the money!"

Jesus always had the material substance He needed to do whatever the Father led Him to do.

Jesus enjoyed the luxury of expensive anointing oils, fine coats, and the needed substance for His traveling Bible college that many times exceeded 5,000 men — not counting women and children!

Money could not have been an occasional thing that was put into His lap. It took a steady flow of finances to operate His extensive ministry throughout the Holy Land.

Keep this in mind. Jesus had only one recorded officer in all of this company, a treasurer named Judas Iscariot. His ministry's treasurer (the man who handled the money) was a very expensive treasurer, for Scripture tells us he was a thief!

> . . . he was a thief, and had the bag, and bare what was put therein.
>
> **John 12:6b**

Jesus knew Judas was a thief, yet He never fired him! So, not only did Jesus need to have the finances necessary for the daily operation of His great ministry, but He needed to have enough surplus to make up for that which Judas Iscariot was stealing.

Child of God, surely you must know that it would take substantial finances for a ministry to operate if the treasurer was stealing from every offering!

Do not mistake this tolerance of Judas as Jesus approving of thievery. Judas was allowed to remain in his position so that Jesus could prove a greater truth than "not stealing." You see, I believe that Jesus allowed this to continue to prove that there was more than enough, and because of this knowledge, no financial problem ever arose that He could not meet.

The Bible *never* states the Jesus did without food or basic necessities unless He was fasting or seeking an invitation to stay the night with those whom He hoped to teach and recruit. The record shows that He could afford to send disciples out to *buy* any needed supplies:

> **For his disciples were gone away unto the city to *buy* meat.**
>
> **John 4:8**

Notice, the Word says "to buy," not to beg, for food. When I mentioned that Jesus had fine clothes, I do not draw that conclusion from the pictures I have seen drawn of Him. I arrive at this conclusion based upon knowledge of the Scripture. The Bible states that at His crucifixion, the Roman soldiers drew lots to see who would be the lucky one to receive the fine cloak that Jesus wore. They drew lots because they were afraid the valuable cloak would be torn apart or damaged if they fought over it. The coat was made "without seam," which meant it was woven as one piece of material; only the most expensive clothing of that day was made in this fashion.

> **Now the coat was without seam, woven from the top throughout.**
>
> **They said therefore among themselves, Let us not rend it, but cast lots for it, whose it shall be.**
>
> **John 19:23b,24a**

Do not think that Jesus didn't use the wealth of the wicked to finance His ministry. The wives of some of His enemies gave great sums into the treasury of His ministry.

> **And certain women, which had been healed of evil spirits and infirmities, Mary called Magdalene, out of whom went seven devils,**
>
> **And Joanna the wife of Chuza Herod's steward, and Susanna, and many others,** *which ministered unto him of their substance.*
>
> **Luke 8:2,3**

Notice that Joanna, the wife of Chuza the steward of Herod (keeper of his wealth), ministered unto him of her (and her husband's) substance. In plain English, she gave money to the ministry of Jesus.

Please do not let this next statement throw you. As strange as it may seem to you, it is true: the very first miracle Jesus ever performed was a miracle of *pure luxury.*

Yes, He healed the sick, He brought the dead back to life, He literally walked on water, but the record clearly shows that His *first miracle* was a miracle of pure luxury.

The Bible states that His *first* miracle was the changing of water into wine at the wedding feast. When he performed this first miracle, Jesus showed that He did not care only about people's basic needs, but He also wished to supply their wants, even if they were clearly a luxury and not a bare necessity.

He truly was concerned about us in spirit, soul, and body. This concern for us manifested itself again when Jesus sent His disciples into *the world, not to Israel* (be very careful not to make a mistake on this point). The commission I now speak of is His *second commission.* Jesus gave His disciples a detailed list of things to take (I say again, do not confuse this with His instructions to the disciples when He ministered in Israel).

He had a very realistic attitude about what they would need and how they were to obtain it for the *second commission.*

> **And he said unto them, When I sent you without purse, and scrip, and shoes, lacked ye any thing? And they said, Nothing** [that's when they ministered in Israel].
>
> **Then said he unto them, But *now*** [since they were going into the world] **he that hath a purse, let him take it, and likewise his scrip: and he that hath no sword, let him *sell* his garment, and *buy* one.**
>
> **Luke 22:35,36**

Jesus knew that for His disciples to be able to function effectively in the harsh reality of the world, they would need to be properly equipped. Jesus did not send the church or any of its members or ministries out into the world without proper equipment.

With this statement, Jesus showed that He thoroughly understood the principles of commerce, and approved of His disciples using them.

He clearly instructed them to *sell* their excess so that they could *buy* the equipment that they needed. Notice that He did not say, "If you don't have a sword, *just learn to do without one,*" or, "Wait until I drop one out of heaven for you."

Instead, Jesus told them to operate in the principles dictated by the commerce of their day, and extract from that economy the money they needed to buy equipment.

In today's world, our pastors, our missionaries, and our various other members of the fivefold ministry need the proper equipment and facilities (expensive equipment and facilities, I might add) to bring the saving message of Jesus Christ to the billions of lost souls throughout the whole world.

We must, as quickly as possible, reach these lost souls through every avenue available to us.

We must use to their fullest capacity, the radio programs, television specials, 24-hour-a-day Christian satellite broadcasting, and greatly intensified church soul-winning programs, plus expand needed literature programs.

Tens of thousands of new churches must be started, buildings must be built, and most pressing, all of *the tremendous debts of the existing churches must be paid off.* All of these immediate needs of the endtime church cost vast sums of money.

Why am I saying all of this? Not just to present a negative report of our many needs, but to make the *key point:*

If Jesus were walking the earth today, and if He were giving us the Great Commission of Luke 22:35,36 at this time, He would insist that *all* of His disciples go forth with the proper equipment! He would no doubt command us to use high-tech equipment, radio, television, tapes, computers, and learn how to mass market our message of life to the world.

Throughout the entire Word of God, you will never find an example of a minister of God going forth without the Lord providing a plan to supply the physical needs of that ministry.

God does not hesitate to supply His messengers, His ministers, and His people with all the equipment and supplies that they need to properly work the mighty works of God. If they can learn to operate in the principles of Biblical economics that He clearly teaches in His Word, the needed finances will come forth to purchase any and all of the needed ministry tools and technology.

I hope that you can see that there is more than enough wealth in the world right now to bring the entire world to Jesus. I also hope that by this time you realize that the wicked have it. Finally, I hope it has become clear to you that God plans to take that wealth and give it to His children. It is obvious why He is doing this; so that they can abundantly fund every need of every church and ministry that participates in the great endtime harvest that is before us.

8

God's Pattern of Giving the Wealth of the Wicked to His Children

I believe you are receiving a new insight into the nature of God. It should be no surprise to us when God blesses His children spiritually.

Child of God, you will see in this chapter that it is also His nature to abundantly bless His children in the *material realm* as well!

As you add to your storehouse of knowledge concerning God's standard operating procedures, you will begin to discover that it is an ongoing, established, standard practice throughout history for God to fulfill the second part of Proverbs 13:22b, and transfer the wealth of the wicked to His children at the critical time of their need:

> ... **and the wealth of the sinner** [wicked] **is laid up for the just.**
>
> **Proverbs 13:22b**

Child of God, I can hear your spirit saying, "Brother John, I believe you. I believe you because I believe the Word of God. It says that the wealth of the wicked is laid up for the just, so it must be true. But being a human, my logical mind says this is all just too fantastic to be fulfilled. I have to confess that it is beyond my realm of experience. Yes, I believe the Bible, but I must be totally honest. I have never heard of the wealth being turned over in wholesale fashion to the righteous.

I see from my experience that lost wicked men simply do not give away their wealth."

Child of God, be at ease. You *have heard of this happening* time and time again. Let me now bring some of these times back to your remembrance.

How about Abram and the Egyptians? Do you remember that account in the twelfth chapter of Genesis? Abram received great wealth from the wicked Egyptians.

Keep in mind that Abram was flat broke when he arrived in Egypt. Although it can be argued that he came from rich ancestors, when he and Sarai arrived in Egypt, he definitely was not rich. Upon entering Egypt, he told his wife, Sarai, to tell everyone she met that she was his sister.

Well, you know the story. Pharaoh fell in love with Sarai, and stated that he would marry her on a certain date. The Scriptures says:

> **And he** [the Pharaoh] **entreated Abram well for her sake: and he had sheep, and oxen, and he asses, and menservants, and maidservants, and she asses, and camels.**
>
> **Genesis 12:16**

This was all well and good until the Pharaoh discovered Sarai was really Abram's wife. The Pharaoh became so angry that he threw Abram out of Egypt. Note a very interesting point — Pharaoh let Abram keep all of the wealth he had given him!

> **And Pharaoh commanded his men concerning him: and they sent him away, and his wife, and *all that he had.***
>
> **Genesis 12:20**

Notice that in one short visit to Egypt, the wealth of the wicked was quickly transferred to the just man — Abram. Notice how much wealth Abram acquired in this short time. Chapter 13, verse 2, tells us that upon Abram's departure from Egypt he had great substance:

> **And Abram was *very rich* in *cattle,* in *silver,* and in *gold.***
>
> **Genesis 13:2**

God sent Abram, who just a short time before entered Egypt poor, out of Egypt with an abundance of cattle, silver and gold! Abram was actually *given* the wealth of wicked Egypt.

Further along in this passage, we see that Abram and Lot had acquired *so many possessions* while in Egypt that. . . **the land was not able to bear them.** (Gen. 13:6.)

They actually had such great substance that they could not dwell close together, for they needed large amounts of land to contain and sustain their great herds.

A close examination of Scripture seems to show that Lot's wealth came from his association with Abram. It is important to notice here that Abram's wealth was so abundant and excessive that even his nephew was able to prosper from his vast abundance. Clearly, this shows that when God distributes the wealth, He doesn't mind if His children have more than enough.

Notice, however, that Lot was unable to grasp that the wealth he had been receiving was from God's hands to him. He associated his wealth with the world's economic principles working in his life. Yet, in Genesis 13:14,15 God tells Abram:

> ...Lift up now thine eyes, and look from the place where thou art northward, and southward, and eastward, and westward:
>
> For all the land which thou seest, to thee will I give it, and to thy seed for ever.
>
> **Genesis 13:14,15**

These are not the promises of a God who wants His children to dwell in poverty, starvation and ignorance! No indeed! The God of Abram *is the God of abundance!* In verse 17, God tells Abram:

> Arise, walk through the land in the length of it and in the breadth of it; for I will give it unto thee.
>
> **Genesis 13:17**

That is not a God who wants His people to barely make it! He gave Abram *more than enough!*

Child of God, as you study God's Word carefully, you will find that God's clearly stated intention is to take very good care of His children, especially those who walk in His footsteps and obey His will.

Also, keep in mind that God gave all of this land to Abram and his seed (the righteous). Remember that every bit of this property was once owned by wicked heathen men, and God took that land of the wicked and gave it to the just. Isn't that what we are finding more and more in our study? The wealth of the wicked is laid up for the just.

Let us now look at another case where the wealth of the wicked was transferred to the just.

Let us observe this process as it operated in the life of Isaac. He too experienced the God-ordained transfer of the wealth of the wicked into his possession.

While Isaac was living in his homeland, Genesis 26 tells us that he ran out of supplies because of a harsh famine, so he decided to do as his father before him had done, and go down into Egypt.

Isaac got as far as the land of the Philistines, when God told him to stop.

God told Isaac to stay out of Egypt, and to continue dwelling in the land of the wicked Philistines, a land that the famine had rendered barren and seemingly non-productive.

But God promised Isaac that if he followed His instructions (instructions you and I would probably label as "foolish"), he would prosper.

> **Sojourn in this land, and I will be with thee, and will bless thee; for unto thee, and unto thy seed, I will give all these countries, and I will perform the oath which I swore unto Abraham thy father.**
> **Genesis 26:3**

Some will read this passage and immediately assume that God meant an abundance of *spiritual blessings.* Oh, how we love to give our own definition to God's Word. In verse 12 of this passage, we see what God means by "blessings" in the midst of a famine.

> **Then Isaac sowed in that land** [a land in the midst of famine], **and received in the same year an hundredfold: and the Lord blessed him.**
> **Genesis 26:12**

In verse 14, we see a further inventory of what God had given to Isaac.

> **For he had possession of** *flocks,* **and possession of** *herds,* **and great** *store of servants:* **and** *the Philistines envied him.*
>
> **Genesis 26:14**

Are we to believe that the Philistines envied Isaac's spiritual heritage? Weigh that thought carefully.

Are we to believe that they envied Isaac's good standing with God? Weigh that thought carefully.

Of course not!

The Philistines envied Isaac because he had huge crops for food in the midst of famine — crops that he was able to sell for huge amounts of money to buy large flocks of sheep for meat and for clothing, and because he had a "great store" of servants to wait on his every need. In the midst of famine, Isaac cleaned out the wealth of the Philistines.

That's why the Philistines envied Isaac! He was the son of a living God who prospers His sons and daughters by giving them the wealth of the wicked.

Yes, of course Isaac first and foremost had a deep *spiritual inheritance.* But there was, in like fashion in the natural realm, an abundant *material, earthly inheritance* that God had earmarked for Isaac — the same way He wanted it for Abram.

That's the same way He wants it for you now:

> **Every man also to whom God hath given riches and wealth, and hath given him power to eat thereof, and to** *take his portion,* **and to rejoice in his labour;** *this is the gift of God.*
>
> **Ecclesiastes 5:19**

God gives both *spiritual and financial* wealth to His people.

Poverty is simply not a Biblical principle that applies to the obedient and industrious saints of God. It is time that Christians stop claiming that poverty is what God wants for their lives!

Friend, let's face it, *poverty is not God's perfect will for you.* To live daily on the brink of insufficiency and claim that it is God's intended status for you is a spiritual mistake. In Biblical illustration after Biblical illustration, the same truth keeps emerging:

God has a people, and God takes care of His people, in *the spiritual realm*, in *the physical realm*, and in *the financial realm*.

Hear the beloved Apostle John declare it:

> **Beloved, I wish above all things that thou mayest**
> ***prosper*** **and** *be in health,* **even** *as thy soul prospereth.*
> **3 John 2**

In the 31st chapter of Genesis, we *once again* see this principle of taking the wealth of the wicked and giving it to the just illustrated in the life of Jacob. If you are plagued by a crooked or unsympathetic boss who you believe hinders God's ability to flow His abundance into your life — then read this next section closely!

No one had a more crooked, stingy, unsympathetic boss than Jacob. Laban was crooked, crooked, crooked, and, he was a real tightwad! Ten times, Laban changed Jacob's compensation program! Once, Jacob worked seven years to marry Laban's beautiful daughter, only to have Laban secretly switch daughters at the wedding, and trick Jacob into a marriage with his plain daughter.

After many years of Jacob working faithfully for Laban, God instructed Jacob to "return to the land of thy fathers."

Naturally, Jacob was willing to obey.

But before he left, Jacob revealed to Laban's daughters the amazing divine principle of taking the wealth of the wicked and giving it to the just, the principle that had been operating in his life as he worked for their father Laban.

Read these verses very carefully, for they provide a major breakthrough to understanding the mind of God, and to destroying any previous conceptions you may have about what God will do for His children.

> **And ye know that with all my power I have served your father.**
>
> **And your father hath deceived me, and changed my wages ten times;** *but God suffered him not to hurt me.*
>
> **If he said thus, the speckled shall be thy wages; then all the cattle bare speckled: and if he said thus, The ringstraked shall be thy hire; then bare all the cattle ringstraked.**
>
> **Thus God** *hath taken away the cattle of your father, and given them to me.*
>
> **Genesis 31:6-9**

God took the wealth of Laban (a wicked man who kept changing the rules of Jacob's compensation program) and gave his wealth to Jacob!

Laban could do nothing to stop the transfer of his wealth to Jacob, once God started the process.

When Laban said he would pay Jacob only in the speckled cattle that came forth from the herd, God made all the cattle have speckled young. When Laban said he would only pay in striped cattle, then God made all the calves striped.

God took the wealth of wicked Laban and gave it to just Jacob. And the God of Jacob yesterday is the very same God you serve today and your children will serve tomorrow.

The groundwork for the Lord's abundance in Jacob's life had been laid way back in Genesis 28:20-22. In these verses, Jacob says:

> **And Jacob vowed a vow, saying, If God will be with me, and will keep me in this way that I go, and will give me bread to eat, and raiment to put on,**
>
> **So that I come again to my father's house in peace; then shall the Lord be my God:**
>
> **And this stone, which I have set for a pillar, shall be God's house: and of all that thou shalt give me I will surely *give* the tenth unto thee.**

Jacob clearly covenanted with God that if He would bless him, then surely he (Jacob) would give a tenth of all he received back to God.

Many people construe this vow to mean that Jacob would then begin to tithe, but that simply is not the case. In the book of Hebrews, we see that Israel (Jacob's new name) had tithed in the loins of Abraham.

> **And verily they that are of the sons of Levi, who receive the office of the priesthood, have a command-**

> ment to *take* tithes of the people according to the law,
> that is, of their brethren, though they come out of the
> loins of Abraham.
>
> Hebrews 7:5

All of the seed of Abraham were already tithers. Jacob's promise to God was not that he would become a tither after God blessed him, he already was tithing! Remember, Jacob was the one of the two sons of Isaac who sought after the things of God. Surely, he was a tither from his early years.

Jacob told God he would *"give"* Him ten percent. The tithe is not something we *give* to God; it is something we owe to God, for it is *His* to take.

> And all the tithe of the land, whether of the seed
> of the land, or of the fruit of the tree, is the Lord's:
> it is holy unto the Lord.
>
> Leviticus 27:30

Jacob was vowing with God to "give" him ten percent *over* and above his tithe, in appreciation for the abundant blessings of God.

He established a generous measure of return from God by the generous measure of the offerings he gave to God over and above the tithe. And immediately, because of his faithful tithe, God opened to him the windows of heaven and poured out a blessing to Jacob according to the measure of Jacob's abundant offering. Jacob's offering, not his tithe, determined the amount God returned to him:

> Give, and it shall be given unto you; good
> measure, pressed down, and shaken together, and
> running over, shall men give into your bosom. *For*

> **with the same measure that ye mete withal it shall be measured to you again.**
>
> **Luke 6:38**

Jacob was fortunate to live in a *special period of time* when God was releasing great portions of the wealth of the wicked to the just, for Jacob's sons were the beginning of the twelve tribes of Israel, and they needed to be established.

Abram also operated in a special cycle, a *special period of time* when riches poured forth from the coffers of the wicked to the coffers of the just.

Isaac operated in a similar *special period of time.*

The Bible says that it happened to Abram! It happened to Isaac! It happened to Jacob!

Each one of these great men of God saw the wealth (hard assets) of the wicked transferred from the wicked and placed into his hands.

The same amazing process happened again right at the beginning of the Christian era.

Did you know when, in the last 1900 years, God took the greatest amount of the wealth of the wicked and gave that wealth to His sons and daughters to spread the Gospel throughout the entire world?

It happened during the reign of Constantine the Great, ruler of both the eastern and western Roman Empires from 312 to 337 A.D. In the early part of his life, Constantine slaughtered Christians and fed them to the lions. Surely he qualified as a wicked man at the helm of a very wicked nation.

But one day God, in His grace, gave this ruthless murderer a vision in the sky, and instructed him to go and conquer in the name of God.

Virtually overnight the greater part of the world entered into Christianity.

Virtually overnight the great *wealth of the Roman Empire started to flow into the hands of the Christians.*

Oh, maybe it was not the tongue talking, devil-chasing, on-fire Christianity of the early apostles, but God still gave the wealth of the wicked to His children!

In 313 A.D., Constantine issued a law that would change the course of human history, the Edict of Milan, which for the first time legalized Christianity in the Roman Empire. *All* the power of Rome suddenly became the *power of the church!*

Every part of the known world was touched by this "new doctrine" of Jesus Christ, and His willingness to save sinners. The wealth and resources of the Roman Empire were now at the disposal of the church.

You will be glad to know that on his deathbed, in 337 A.D. Constantine himself finally became a Christian!

Now, child of God, notice very carefully that with the transfer of the wealth of the Roman Empire to Christianity, the objection that many well-meaning, uninformed critics of this message bring up is put to rest. They say: "These Scriptures of the transfer of the wicked's wealth are purely Old Testament, and do not apply to New Testament times."

I leave the decision up to you.

Is 313 A.D. New Testament times or not?

Surely it is, and with this great event this concept jumps the boundary between Old and New Testaments, and brings this truth right into our day. Remember, God is the same throughout history, yesterday, today, and forever!

The Chosen People Take Egypt's Wealth!

Before I end this chapter, let me highlight one final, powerful example of how God takes the wealth of the wicked and freely gives that wealth to the just.

Israel was in bondage for 400 years. For 400 years, Israel was poorer than poor. Then God said, "Let my people go." How could this poverty-ridden nation, without a substantial economic base, ever bring forth the great revelation of God's law, the structure of God's government as we find it in Exodus, Leviticus, Numbers, and Deuteronomy?

Let us start at the beginning of Exodus, when God decided to release this nation from the iron fist of Egypt's bondage. Egypt, through the Pharaoh, had a hold on Israel that was so tight and so humanly impossible to break that Scripture refers to Israel's captivity as an iron furnace:

> **But the Lord hath taken you, and brought you forth out of *the iron furnace.***
> **Deuteronomy 4:20a**

In the case of Israel's release from captivity, we see that God used Moses as His man for this great cycle of the release of the wealth of the wicked into the hands of the just.

Twelve plagues came in successive waves from God, from a rod turning to a serpent, to the rivers of Egypt turning to blood, to frogs infesting the land, to lice-like clouds of dust, and to flies so thick that they swarmed until the land was ruined. Then disease came on all the flocks of Egypt, and sore boils covered all of the citizens and animals of Egypt from head to foot. Next the cattle of Egypt were stricken with disease; then hail and fire were mingled together to ravage the land. Then hoards of locusts came, followed by the judgment of thick darkness.

Each of these judgments came with no release for God's people!

Finally, God moved in what is no doubt the most powerful judgment since the flood of Noah. The twelfth judgment came in on the wings of the dreaded death angel of God, sweeping across Egypt, taking the lives of every firstborn of men and beasts of Egypt.

Keep in mind that none of these judgments came upon any of the children of Israel. Now, on the eve of the greatest of these judgments, God came to Moses with very strange instructions.

> **And the Lord said unto Moses, Yet will I bring one plague more upon Pharaoh, and upon Egypt; afterwards he will let you go hence: when he shall let you go, he shall surely thrust you out hence altogether.**
>
> **Speak now in the ears of the people, and let every man borrow of his neighbor, and every woman of her neighbor, jewels of silver, and jewels of gold.**
>
> **And the Lord gave the people favour in the sight of the Egyptians.**
>
> **Exodus 11:1-3a**

> **And the children of Israel did according to the word of Moses; and they borrowed of the Egyptians jewels of silver, and jewels of gold, and raiment:**
>
> **And the Lord gave the people favour in the sight of the Egyptians, so that they lent unto them such things as they required. And they spoiled the Egyptians.**
>
> **Exodus 12:35,36**

Child of God, are you seeing the miracle here? Egypt was full of the dead firstborn of all living things; there were rivers of blood, lice, and boils everywhere, and here came the unscathed Israelites, asking these bewildered, defeated Egyptians, "By the way, before we leave here, can we please borrow all of your gold and silver and valuables?"

And the Egyptians *freely gave* all their gold, silver, and other precious possessions.

What a miracle! When Israel came out of bondage, Exodus 12:37 says they numbered about 600,000 men. If you add wives and children, probably more than three and a half million Israelites left Egypt, but mind you, not as slaves!

There were three and a half million millionaires heading for the desert, equipped with virtually everything they needed. The Word tells us that the Israelites were so rich, and the Egyptians now so poor, that the wealth of the Israelites tempted the Egyptians to follow them into the parted Red Sea. (Did you ever wonder what possessed the Egyptians to dare to enter the watery, walled canyon that crossed the Red Sea?)

We know the Egyptians were after the Israelite's newly acquired wealth from Exodus 15:9a:

**The enemy said, I will pursue, I will overtake,
I will *divide the spoil*....**

After 400 years of poverty, the children of Israel were now rich. They had great wealth. *But let the depth of this truth come forth* — God had given the Israelites the wealth of the wicked of Egypt, and yet, there was absolutely nothing in the wilderness to spend that wealth on!

No stores. No shopping centers. And best of all, no personal needs. They had gold, yet they never (for forty years) needed to buy food. They had silver, yet their clothes never wore out!

Out in the wilderness, there was no place to spend money. They had manna and quail to eat, water to drink, and light from the pillar of fire by night.

Now get the *real* purpose for God giving the wealth of the wicked to the children of God. The only thing they could use the gold and silver for (the wealth of wicked Egypt that God had just given them) was to build the tabernacle in the wilderness!

...and I will prepare him an habitation.
Exodus. 15:2b

God wanted them to take the gold and silver of the wicked wealthy Egyptians not to lavish upon themselves, but that they might build Him a dwelling place in their midst.

Child of God, get this point, and get it well. The wealth of heathen Egypt was for the building of the dwelling place of God. The value of that great building with its gold and silver, and the precious woods, jewels, and so on was astronomical. But you cannot help but notice the parallel of these former days with the last days in which we now dwell in.

This time, God is giving us the wealth of the wicked so we can build Him a temple, a holy habitation *not made with hands,* but one made with lively stones. This endtime temple is not a mortar and stone building. It is the church of the Lord Jesus Christ made of human bodies of the redeemed who are the true temple of the living God, the dwelling place of God Jehovah.

Yes, God took the wealth of Egypt (the wicked, wealthy world) and gave it to the Israel of old (we are the present-day Israel of God) to build Him a tabernacle in the wilderness. And later on, with the wealth that King David took from the wicked of his day, they built a great temple at Jerusalem (both were built with the wealth of the wicked, and both were acquired by the children of God).

9

The Wealth of the Wicked
Is Given to God's Children
at Specific Times

These men of God we have been discussing *all* operated in a *special period of time,* a time when God gave huge amounts of the wealth of the wicked to His people in order to establish them and His message in the earth.

These Biblical examples should clearly show you that it *is* part of God's nature, it *is* part of God's normal process, it *is* His habitual method of operation, to abundantly bless His People from the coffers of the wealthy wicked.

Many of you might be wondering why you have not heard this before. You may be asking, "Why doesn't my church denomination teach this truth?"

Child of God, there are two levels of comprehending God's Word:

1. Knowing the ways of God, the "whys" of Scripture, and,

2. Knowing the acts of God, the "what" of Scripture.

In Psalm 103:7, there is an important truth you need to grasp to understand these Biblical concepts, and to have them continue to grow in your spirit.

> **He made** *known his ways* **unto Moses,** *his acts*
> **unto the children of Israel.**
>
> **Psalm 103:7**

I pray that you, as my reader, are one of those who *knows his ways* instead of only His acts.

Many of the saints today easily can see and attest to the acts of God, like the children of Israel, but there are a few choice saints with the type of advanced revelatory knowledge that Moses had who *know* and *understand* the very *ways* of God.

These informed, enlightened sons and daughters of God know that:

1. God wants to bless His children abundantly right from the wealth of the wicked, in certain cycles and in certain situations at strategic times.

2. During these times, God will *take away* the wealth from the wicked, and redistribute that wealth among the just to build and rapidly expand the Kingdom of God.

Child of God, hear me close on this.

I am *not* revealing to you the typical Christian prosperity message that is so frequently being taught in our churches and in the Christian media (though that is a valid message, and is ordained by God!)

Please understand the significance of what is being said here. This is a *revelation* that goes beyond the general teachings of prosperity and enters into a special time cycle for releasing the wealth of the wicked again *in our time, into our hands.*

This is a unique prophecy for a special people in a *special period of time!*

You say, "What is so special about this time?"

Child of God, this is the endtime hour, and God is going to transfer the wealth of the wicked to the just during this final cycle.

God is once again, in the end of this age, going to do something, something completely consistent with His nature, to finance the final gathering of His endtime harvest.

God will take away the wealth from the wicked, and bestow the control of that wealth into the hands of the just, the Israel of God, His blood-bought children who are ready and willing to use that wealth for His final, endtime harvest. We, the redeemed of God, are His endtime temple, not some reconstruction of an ancient temple made with hands, but a living, holy habitation, made up of redeemed human beings!

> . . . for ye are the temple of the living God; as God hath said, I will dwell in them, and walk in them; and I will be their God, and they shall be my people.
> 2 Corinthians 6:16b

This revelation is not talking about Christians getting money to lavish upon themselves.

This revelation is not talking about you getting bigger homes, fancier swimming pools, and more vacations (again, these are consistent with a legitimate message in God's Word, but that's not the message of this book).

The revelation that this book speaks of is God's chosen people, now in the Endtimes, becoming prepared to liberally redistribute the wealth of the wicked to the places that God directs. This will be a people whose first and foremost desire is to finance the final endtime harvest of souls.

Remember, it is God who gives His children the power to get wealth to establish His covenant:

> **But thou shalt remember the Lord thy God: for it is he that giveth thee power to get wealth, that he may establish his covenant which he sware unto thy fathers, as it is this day.**
>
> **Deuteronomy 8:18**

God has given you the power to extract that wealth from the wealthy wicked.

> **Give, and it shall be given unto you; good measure, pressed down, and shaken together, and running over, shall men** [primarily lost men] **give into your bosom.**
>
> **Luke 6:38a**

Timing is of the utmost importance in being successful in any warfare, especially spiritual warfare. Jesus Himself tells us of the peril of not discerning the times:

> **The Pharisees also with the Sadducees came, and tempting desired him that he would shew them a sign from heaven.**
>
> **He answered and said unto them, When it is evening, ye say, It will be fair weather: for the sky is red.**
>
> **And in the morning, It will be foul weather to day: for the sky is red and lowering.** *O ye hypocrites, ye can discern the face of the sky; but can ye not discern the signs of the times?"*
>
> **Matthew 16:1-3**

The endtime harvest is upon us!

The trumpet will one day sound in this Endtime!

God will complete the work, but only those who discern the times that we are in will be ready to reap the financial harvest of the great endtime transfer of wealth.

Only those who discern the time will be able to effectively fund the great endtime harvest, for even as there were many in Israel who did not discern the time of the first coming of Christ, so too there will be many who will not discern the nature of the endtime return of Christ.

They will be wistfully awaiting a catching away, and thereby they will miss the privilege of participating in the greatest ingathering of souls that the world has ever experienced.

But, thanks be to God, just as there was a group in Israel at His first coming who discerned the times, heralded His appearance, and carried the Good News to the world, there will also be saints in these last days who will be anticipating the endtime harvest of the wealth of the wicked, and they will, by faith, reach out and take it! They will use these funds for the greatest revival and ingathering that has ever happened on planet earth.

I invite you, on the authority of God, to come and join in this special endtime cycle of God. Prepare for the battle. There are many glorious events still ahead for the church as we prepare Him a dwelling in the saints on the earth!

10

No Spoils for Reluctant Saints

Until you know *who* you are in Christ Jesus, the devil will have a virtual field day in your finances. *Until you know* and exercise your authority over him, his devastating raids will continue.

Child of God, I have come to realize that as much as they would like to, most Christians today do not *know* how to defeat Satan in the area of their finances!

They rebuke sickness. They take dominion over every germ and virus. But, try as they may, they cannot keep their finances out of the red. They fail to recognize that it is the devil who is at work in their finances. While they know the doctrine of salvation, and of the indwelling of the Holy Ghost, *they do not know the first thing about the Biblical principles of economics*, and how to apply them to their own personal finances.

In this chapter, I want once and for all to stop Satan's subtle lies to you about your money, and to help you to enter into the *mind of God* about your finances, and experience a powerful *breakthrough* in the area of your personal finances. Let's covenant together right here and now to turn your financial minuses to pluses.

I am praying that you will experience that which God wanted Israel to experience each time they came and went from the temple.

In the days of Old Testament Israel, God urged His people to always come into the temple by one gate, and leave by another:

> **But when the people of the land shall come before the Lord in the solemn feasts, he that entereth in by the way of the north gate to worship shall go out by the way of the south gate; and he that entereth by the way of the south gate shall go forth by the way of the north gate:** *he shall not return by the way of the gate whereby he came in,* **but shall go forth over against it.**
> **Ezekiel 46:9**

Why do you suppose God wanted it that way? Because God did not want the Israelites to leave His house the same way they came in.

Today, that's my prayer for you.

No matter how you *enter* this chapter, no matter how deeply and how subtly Satan's lies about your finances have permeated your spirit, I pray right now that the mighty *power* of the Holy Spirit will enable you to *leave* this chapter, *renewed in the mind of God*, with all the old lies destroyed, and with a *fresh new ability* to apply God's principles of economics in your life.

I want you to leave this chapter financially different from how you entered it. Let's begin by stating clearly God's wish for your life:

> **Beloved, I wish above all things that thou mayest** *prosper* **and** *be in health*, **even as** *thy soul prospereth*.
> **3 John 2**

When God speaks of your *"soul's prosperity,"* His desire is that you prosper in all of your spiritual matters. God desires that you come to *know* Him in a deeply personal way, and that you *use* the spiritual gifts and procedures He has provided for you more skillfully each day.

When God speaks of your *"health,"* His desire for you is that you eat the foods that will nourish your body; that you take proper exercise, and avoid those physical excesses that will harm your total health, and that the stripes of Jesus work against all of the germs and viruses that threaten your good health every day.

Note this carefully: when God clearly says He wants you (each individual saint) to *"prosper,"* He is speaking concerning the day-to-day matters of your money and your material wealth.

You see, God wants you to prosper in all three of these areas:

1. Your spiritual walk

2. Your health

3. *Your possessions*

Since we have already established that there is more than enough wealth in God's abundant world, and since we have already established that in these Endtimes, God is declaring that the wealth of the wicked is going to be literally transferred into the hands of Christians, it is now vitally important for you to know that God has actually *empowered you* to seize that wealth.

Deuteronomy 8:18 provides the Scriptural foundation:

> **But thou shalt remember the Lord thy God: for it is he that giveth thee *power to get wealth*,**

that he may establish his covenant which he sware unto thy fathers, as it is this day.
Deuteronomy 8:18

Many of you still cannot believe what you are reading in this verse, but it clearly states that God gives *you* the *supernatural power* to get wealth, power that goes beyond your natural abilities to take control of such hard assets as money, lands, stocks and bonds — not in some distant future life, but right now, in this life!

If God has really given Christians the *power* to get wealth to establish His covenant (and bring in the end-time harvest), then why aren't more Christians operating in this supernatural ability to get wealth?

I am convinced that most Christians are willing to believe God's Word, *but they have trouble fully believing and trusting the men of God who teach them God's Word.*

Child of God, if you ever plan to release the God-ordained prosperity for your life, you must learn how to believe God's prophets who teach you the Word of God.

You have probably read or heard many times about the Biblical account concerning the little widow at Zarephath. You probably remember how she only had a little meal left, and was about to eat her last nourishment.

Elijah arrived at her house and asked for a cake. First, the little widow said no; then she finally agreed to bake Elijah a cake.

You know the details of this story, but let me now share with you a few key things you may not realize concerning the relationship between the widow and Elijah.

When the widow first saw Elijah, it was not the first time she had ever heard about him. God had already told her Elijah was coming, and that she was to feed him!

And the word of the Lord came unto him, saying,

Arise, get thee to Zarephath, which belongeth to Zidon, and dwell there: behold, *I have commanded a widow woman there to sustain thee.*
1 Kings 17:8,9

Do you see how fortunate this widow woman was? God had spoken to her! Yet, even though God spoke to her, and *commanded* her to take care of Elijah — she still was not willing to obey God by sharing her assets with the man of God.

Isn't that interesting? This woman received that which most people desire — God literally spoke to her; He actually commanded her — yet she was not willing to do what God said.

Do you see a spiritual truth here?

Just because God speaks to you does not necessarily mean you will obey. When God speaks to you to give an amount of money into the offering and you refuse, you do two things to help the spirit of shortage to survive in the earth. First of all, you cut off God's blessings of money to the ministry or person God directed your money to. Beyond that, you block the abundant financial miracles God had in store for your finances.

Obedience to God — and the men of God — is a key spiritual truth for receiving God's abundant financial blessings in your life. The widow heard from God, but, hear the powerful truth of this verse: she did not obey *until she heard from the man of God.*

Her much-needed supply could not be released until she obeyed!

When Elijah told the widow, **Bring me, I pray thee, a morsel of bread in thine hand** (1 Kings 17:11), the widow became furious!

She gave Elijah four excuses *why* she could not fetch the bread for him:

- Excuse One: No Cake

    And she said, As the Lord thy God liveth, I have not a cake...

- Excuse Two: Shortage of meal

    But an handful of meal in a barrel...

- Excuse Three: Little oil

    And a little oil in a cruse: and, behold, I am gathering two sticks, that I may go in and dress it...

- Excuse Four: No surplus

    For me and my son, that we may eat it, and die.
    1 Kings 17:12

The widow exploded excuses at Elijah! She got "technical" with him. Have you ever done that with a man of God? Have you ever said, "Well, pastor, I'd love to give to the building fund, but I simply do not have the money right now. There's the house payment, plus the stock market is slow, and besides, all my extra money is tied up in long-term interest accounts."

How often we get "technical" with God or the man of God, in the area of our finances, "I can't give any money this month, pastor, because I've got to get new tires for the car."

For the widow, "being technical" involved her claim to not have bread. Yet she *had the ingredients to make bread!* The widow did not fool God's man, for actually she wasn't attempting to fool him, she was attempting to fool God. Remember, Ananias and Sapphira spoke only to the Apostle Peter, yet Peter said that they had lied to the Holy Ghost:

> **But Peter said, Ananias, why hath Satan filled thine heart to lie to the Holy Ghost?**
>
> **Acts 5:3a**

Child of God, when the little widow woman gave Elijah all of her excuses, look at the first thing he said:

> **And Elijah said unto her, *Fear not; go and do as thou hast said:* but make me thereof a little cake first, and bring it unto me, and after make for thee and for thy son.**
>
> **1 Kings 17:13**

Fear not! Do what God is leading you to do! If he tells you to give to the church building fund, then give. Do not allow fear to dictate in your financial matters before God. If He tells you to give to a Christian telethon, then give to that outreach.

Look what else Elijah told the widow. *Go and do as thou hast said* (v.13).

The Wealth of the World

Buy the tires for the car. Take that vacation you have had planned. But first, give to God what He expects you to give, and *all those other things will be added to you!*

Elijah tells the widow not to let *fear* disqualify her from that which God has for her. Elijah commands her, with full confidence as God's man, to give, and then encourages her to *still* plan to do the things she wanted to do. "Plan to have a cake for you and your son."

Child of God, your heavenly Father *is not going to rain on your picnic.* He does not want you to do without. He wants you to have enough faith to give, and enough faith to believe that your giving to Him will not mess up your prior plans for tires, cars, houses, or whatever else you need.

Give to God what He says to give, and then just go on with even greater confidence in His ability to accomplish the things He promises, knowing that He will not sacrifice *your needs* for *his desires.*

Why did this widow prosper? *Because she obeyed the prophet of God!* Even though God Himself had spoken to her *before* Elijah arrived in Zarephath. Notice, God's personal words to her were not bringing her the needed blessing. God had clearly commanded her to sustain Elijah, but she stubbornly refused to move on God's Word alone.

She finally moved when the man of God respoke the words that God had previously spoken to her. Note that she did not obey God until the man of God confirmed the Word of God to her.

118

Now, don't get pious on me. Think of how this truth manifested itself in your own salvation. God called most of us many times before we responded. And what about receiving the Holy Spirit? Didn't it take more than just one nudge by the Holy Spirit? Many ignore the call to preach for years. It is very common for man to say no to God!

Then, after saying no to God, when the man of God preaches to us, we surrender and commit our lives to salvation, to receiving the Holy Ghost, or to preaching the Gospel.

The same is true of the widow.

She did not obey *until* Elijah ministered the message of giving to her, dealt with her fears, and repeated the promises of God to her in the realm of supply through giving. *Then,* after she believed the prophet, she obeyed, and just look what happened then:

> **For thus saith the Lord God of Israel, The barrel of meal shall not waste, neither shall the cruse of oil fail, until the day that the Lord sendeth rain upon the earth.**
>
> **1 Kings 17:14**

The widow discovered a great spiritual key to prosperity by *obeying* God's man (the prophet); her prosperity was released to her.

But don't take John Avanzini's interpretation of this Scripture as God's final word. Look at the Word of God in yet another place where this principle is made abundantly clear:

> ... **Believe in the Lord your God, so shall ye be established;** [most of today's church members are

firmly established]; **believe his prophets, so shall ye prosper** [most of today's church members look with suspicion on God's prophets, and are in or near poverty].

2 Chronicles 20:20b

God Himself told the widow woman what to do, and she did not do it. But she listened to God's prophet and she prospered! If you were doing *everything* God is telling you to do, you would not need a pastor, you would probably be a pastor! Do not ever think that just because God tells you to do something, you will always do it. His Word is full of things He wants you to do, but most of them only get done when a man of God, empowered and anointed by the Holy Spirit, prompts you to move.

God created your human nature, so He certainly understands what motivates you to action.

You see, the church of God understands the first part of this promise, **Believe in the Lord your God, so shall ye be established,** and the church is firmly entrenched and established in the earth.

But all too few of God's saints understand the consequences of not fulfilling the second half of that verse: **Believe his prophets, so shall ye prosper.**

How many "established" Christians do we have in the world today? Quite a few. Literally millions upon millions throughout the whole world. They are solid in their faith, yet the greater part of them live from day to day, or flounder in or on the brink of poverty.

The greater part of God's church has questions in their hearts about the men of God (the prophets, if you please), and this suspicion of the motives of God's men keeps the saints just out of reach of real prosperity. (I am not advocating that you throw caution to the wind. Please use good sense to discern the true men of God.)

To lay hold of God's prosperity, you've go to start believing His prophets.

Child of God, *believe me.* There are some specific things that God has revealed to me about these Endtimes, and about your finances, that are prophetic. If you lay hold of these revelations and believe God's man, God says that *He will prosper you!*

So, friend of mine, do yourself a favor. If you don't believe this prophet, *then by all means find some man of God you do believe on this subject,* because God says in His Word that your trust relationship with the man of God, or the men of God who bring you the message of God, is strategic in establishing prosperity in your life!

Always keep this in mind when you judge a prophet's validity. A true prophet will always give you a word that is on line *with* the Holy Scriptures, and that prophecy will not disagree with or contradict other parts of God's Word.

The Word of God teaches prosperity.

And every true prophet of God teaches in accordance with the Word of God.

11

Something Is Wrong With Today's Teaching on Tithing

This message of financial abundance is for you, now.

The heaped up treasures of this earth are available to you, now.

God has a specific plan for funding His television ministries, as well as every other agency of His church. The faithful execution of that plan will depend upon our personal finances for proper funding.

But if you activate only 20 percent of God's plan in your life, it will not work. If you perform only 80 percent of God's plan in your life, it will not work.

Hear me, child of God.

God intends to mobilize an endtime army of saints who will take the wealth of the wicked for the harvesting of the world in these last days! These saints will not be 30 percent or 80 percent committed to His principles of Biblical economics. They will be 100 percent dedicated to performing His plan *in detail*.

When you get this same 100 percent dedication, that's when His plan for the transfer of the wealth of the wicked will really start working in your life.

Every place I go, I am confronted with the same story. A little over 20 percent of the church members are tithers. They eagerly tell me how "blessed" they have been by their tithing, "Brother John," they say, "from the day I started tithing, God started blessing my finances."

They excitedly tell me how their bills are all current, how they take a nice vacation each year, how their modest I.R.A. account is growing (at about the same rate as inflation), and how they own a nearly new car, with all the payments current.

This has become the standard interpretation of the passage in Malachi 3:10 that tells us to tithe and God will. . .**open you the windows of heaven, and pour you out a blessing, that there shall not be room enough to receive it.**

Friend of mine, that is a very disappointing interpretation of Malachi 3:10. I am convinced that these saints are not seeing the full effect of the plan of tithing on their income, but merely are experiencing the benefits that good budgeting brings to a person who starts to tithe.

Have you ever met a tither who didn't have a budget? Every tither I know operates on a budget of some sort, and anyone on a budget, including a lost bartender or a dance hall queen, can pay his/her bills if he/she is disciplined in spending by a budget.

Now tell the truth.

You started some kind of a budget when you started tithing, so that your finances began to carefully flow into a proper order. Your "financial blessings" were not the result of spiritual law, but they were the result of the natural law of accounting.

I meet literally tens of thousands of Christians each year, and I have yet to meet a Christian who has told me, "Brother John, since I've been tithing, God has poured me out a blessing I *just can't contain*. Why, I can't hire accountants fast enough to count all the money. I can't buy any more houses or cars, because I've got too many already. Yes, sir, Brother John, the Bible is certainly right. If you tithe, God will pour out a blessing that just cannot be contained."

The literal fulfillment of the *King James* translation of Malachi 3:10 *has not happened*. The abundant expectation of a blessing that cannot be contained is not being manifested in the Body of Christ anywhere in the world today.

In this chapter, I will show you, through God's Word, why that is the case.

I want you to come to a totally *new understanding* about the tithe. I want to assist you in obtaining a financial breakthrough, a breakthrough that will take you beyond just an orderly execution of your financial obligations each month and into a realm of financial breakthrough. A breakthrough that will allow you to have exceedingly abundantly more than enough, so that you can have all of your needs and wants met, and have plenty left over to operate a great ministry of abundant giving to the ministries that you long to support.

Let us begin with a new intensive look at a Scripture you have probably read many times:

> **Will a man rob God? Yet ye have robbed me. But ye say, Wherein have we robbed thee? In *tithes* and *offerings*.**
>
> **Malachi 3:8**

Notice carefully that this verse brings attention to two robberies that God states are taking place:

- *Robbery number one:* The Tithes

- *Robbery number two:* The Offerings

You know that God did not just include "offerings" to balance out the sentence, or to allow the type to go all the way to the margin. Yet, in virtually every sermon or lesson I've heard on this verse, only the tithe is dealt with, and the *offerings* are hardly ever mentioned!

To emphasize this fact, notice that the whole church refers to this section of Scripture as the *"tithing chapter,"* and pastors, evangelists, and teachers alike quote the verses in Malachi to show the Body of Christ that they must tithe.

But *God says* that you have robbed Him in two ways: (1) tithes and (2) offerings.

As a result of these robberies, God says:

> **Ye are cursed with a curse: for ye have robbed me, even this whole nation.**
>
> **Malachi 3:9**

Failure to tithe *and* failure to give offerings *both* result in the curse coming on your finances.

I hope that you are starting to feel a breakthrough stirring in your spirit. Most of you have never really noticed the vital importance of *offerings* in this chapter. With this in mind, let's go on into verse 10:

> **Bring ye all the tithes into the storehouse, that there may be meat in mine house.**
> **Malachi 3:10a**

Does this verse say, "If you tithe, there will be plenty of meat in *your* house?" No!

Yet, that's the mistaken message that has been going out over the pulpits to the Body of Christ for years! In my twenty-five plus years of ministry, countless disappointed tithers have come to me, pleading with me to explain why "the tithe isn't working" in their lives.

Friend of mine, hear me well: the tithe always works! It has never failed even once to do *what God said it would do.*

God always fulfills His promises.

The problem with the tithe not working comes when man fails to understand clearly what God promises that it would do.

God says, "If you tithe, there will be meat [supply] in *My* house [God's house]."

Man has been falsely teaching, "If you tithe, there will be meat in *your* house." (Please understand this clearly in your mind before you go on. I would suggest you get a copy of this Scripture and read it carefully.) Let me also interject at this point that I will not deal at this time with what the tithe is. Neither will I deal with the documentation of the validity of the tithe in the New Testament experience. I do believe that the tithe is valid in all the dispensations. This includes the New Testament.

Now let's look further at Malachi 3:10:

> ...and prove me now herewith, saith the Lord of hosts, if I will not open you the windows of heaven, and pour you out a blessing, that *there shall* not *be room* enough *to receive it.*"

Notice carefully the seven words that are in italic in this text. In the *King James Version,* these seven words appear in italics. The reason that they are printed in italics is to caution the reader that they are reading a word or words that do not appear in the original text.

Do not let this alarm you. It is an accepted practice to add a few words (a very limited amount) when translating from one language to the other — to clarify thoughts that cannot be translated by a one-word equivalent.

Because of this technique in translating, the *King James Version* is excellent for locating words that do not appear in the original text, since the *King James Version* always alerts the reader to added words by italicizing them.

Notice that these words in italics, *there shall be room to receive it,* are added words by the translators, and they do not appear in the original text. (It is interesting to note that in my study of Scripture, I've never found a passage containing more italicized words than Malachi 3:10).

I am not saying it is wrong to have italicized words in a text. Anyone who has ever performed the tedious task of translating from one language to another knows that sometimes there just is not a perfect word fit for a word in the original language. It often takes two words in one language to say what is meant in one word in another language.

Unfortunately, the seven words in this very critical passage, these italicized words in Malachi 3:10, do not clarify the text. Instead, they actually *add a meaning* to the sacred text that *God never intended!*

The original text does not say what is currently found in the *King James Version* of Malachi 3:10. In fact, Malachi never wrote it that way! It is a strict law of translation that whenever translators add words for clarification, they must *never* change the meaning of the original sentence.

In Malachi 3:10, the meaning has been greatly changed.

At this point you may be starting to squirm in your chair. Negative thoughts may be flooding your mind. Satan is trying to *stop this spiritual breakthrough* in your life. He will suggest any lie that keeps you from reading, with any agreement, what the spirit of God is trying to say to you through this book.

Child of God, have faith — for just a moment longer. Press on. Hear me out on this matter. Keep that mind of yours open for growth.

Let God release this abundant financial breakthrough truth in your mind. Let us look at Malachi 3:10 without the seven added words.

> **Bring ye all the tithes into the storehouse, that there may be meat in *mine* house, and prove me now herewith, saith the Lord of hosts, if I will not *open* you**

> **the windows of heaven, and pour you out a blessing, that**
> **not enough.**
>
> **Malachi 3:10**

God tells us that the windows of heaven open, and that He stands ready to pour out blessings.

But, He says, *"That's not enough."* Just opening the windows of heaven is not enough. There is something else to do to make the process complete and fully functional.

All of you know, or you should know by now that *you cannot receive from God without first giving to God.* All of us also know that when we have tithed, we have *not given* anything to God.

When you tithe, you have not *given* God a dime. Failure to tithe is robbery. *Plain and simple, the tithe already belongs to God.*

> **And all the tithe of the land, whether of the seed of**
> **the land, or of the fruit of the tree, is the Lord's: it is holy**
> **unto the Lord.**
>
> **Leviticus 27:30**

The tithe is not *yours* to give to God. If you are still confused, and you think that the tithe is something that you own that you give to God, then look at the next verse:

> **And if a man will at all redeem aught of his tithes, he**
> **shall add thereto the fifth part thereof.**
>
> **Leviticus 27:31**

Do you see it? When you choose to use God's tithe for your own purposes, and say to yourself, "I'll make it up next Sunday," then the Lord says, "You owe Me twenty percent interest on *My* tithe."

Can you imagine how spiritually bankrupt some of the members of the Body of Christ must be? They owe God a full twenty percent interest on all of the tithes they have failed to pay over all the years of their lives!

I just thank God that He didn't come to collect all the debts I owed to Him when I ignorantly kept back His tithe for my own use. Instead, He graciously allowed me to move on to a clean new slate where every debt was already paid by His death on Calvary.

Jesus Christ will do the same in your life the moment you start tithing and set the Biblical laws of economics to work in your finances. He will wipe your slate clean of interest and tithe owed to Him.

When you tithe to God, the Word says two things happen:

1. Meat (supply) goes into God's house (or ministries), and

2. The windows of heaven are *opened* over your life.

Remember, you are not "giving" to God when you tithe, you are simply "returning" what God has given to you. You *owe* God the tithe, and since it is already His, you cannot "give" it to Him.

You can openly be counted as faithful when you freely return it to Him.

Let me illustrate. If you were to loan me your car, and I drove it all around town enjoying the free use of it, when I return it to you at the agreed time, you surely would not reward me or pay me for bringing your car back to you. You will have no reason to "pour me out a blessing" for bringing back the car you so graciously allowed me to use. When I bring it back to you, I've only done that which was expected of me.

When I returned the car, I did not "give" you anything. I owed you the car; it was your property and I have simply brought it back to you. And, you do not *owe* me anything for returning to you that which you have entrusted to me.

In faithfully returning the car to you, I have established a *position of trust* with you. If you can trust me with your car, you might *open* up your house to me, and allow me to stay there the next time I am in town.

That is the *same* principle that the tithe operates in.

God owns *all* the tithe; He leaves it to you to collect from the world system, and He expects you to faithfully return it to Him. When you do this, you have not "given" God anything; but you have, through your honesty, established a *position of trust* with Him.

Tithing simply *opens the windows* of God's abundant supply to you. These open windows then await the giving of *your offering* to establish *the measure* that will be used to flow the blessings of God through those *open windows* of heaven into your control.

Offerings

The reason so many Christians have been frustrated by tithing is because they claim that *when they have tried it, it did not work.*

Of course it worked. Their faithful tithing *opened the windows* of heaven every time they tithed, but in the correct translation of Malachi 3:10, we learn that getting the windows of heaven open and seeing God prepared to give *is not enough!*

It takes one more important step.

Get these two vital truths straight:

Step 1 — The tithe *opens* the windows of heaven.

Step 2 — The offering determines the measure that God will use to flow your blessings through those *open windows* of heaven.

If you have only been tithing, "returning" to God precisely 10 percent of the fruits of your labor, you are literally living under open windows, but you have empty pockets.

You see, it is your *offering* that determines the measure God uses to measure out to you the blessings through the open windows of heaven, windows that your tithe opened.

> **Give, and it shall be given unto you; good measure, pressed down, and shaken together, and running over, shall men give into your bosom. For with the same measure that ye mete withal it shall be measured to you again.**
>
> **Luke 6:38**

Are you starting to see it now? *This is not your standard prosperity message.* I believe God is giving you a breakthrough in this area of finances right now.

God's Word says, **Give, and it shall be given unto you,** but, beloved, you already know that you cannot "give" the tithe. God already owns that. The only thing you can "give" to God is your offerings!

Tithing *opens the windows* of heaven. *Offerings* determine the measure of blessing that flows through the open windows of heaven.

> For with the same measure that ye mete withal,
> it shall be measured to you again.
>
> **Luke 6:38b**

When you tithe, God says, "Okay, I've got My heavenly windows open. I'm ready to start sending you your blessing. What size scoop do you want Me to use?"

If you decide to give a teaspoon offering, God instructs His angels, "Bring me the teaspoon. I've got to return the blessings to My precious child in a teaspoon quantity. A teaspoon is the measure he established in the giving of his offering to Me."

The potential for greater blessing exists.

You may be asking, "Now, Brother John, how do you know God would have to return the blessing with a teaspoon if I give just a small teaspoon offering?"

Because Scripture says, **For with the same measure that ye mete withal, it shall be measured to you again.**

When you start to get serious about applying the Biblical principles of economics in your life, you might decide to start giving by the cupful, because "with the same measure he has measured it to Me, it shall be measured again to him."

Any time you are about to make a spiritual breakthrough, conflicts start happening. The first time you had the courage to open your mouth and allow a heavenly language to pour out, you probably experienced a high level of discomfort and unbelief.

As God's blessings flowed in your life through tongues, your use of this free gift became more and more frequent, and you overcame the hindrances that Satan tried to put in your way.

The same is true of your finances.

We are learning about a spiritual matter when we study the Biblical principles of economics. As you near a breakthrough, Satan will attempt to lie to you.

Your palms may sweat. Tinges of fear and doubt may arise. If you stay strong, soon you will grow to a level of spiritual giving where your cupful and shovelful offerings will be superseded by offerings by the wheelbarrow full.

Then God will tell His angels, "Bring the heavenly wheelbarrows and start dumping out my blessings on that precious saint who is giving those wheelbarrows full of offerings. Pour out those wheelbarrow blessings through those *windows* he continuously keeps open with the faithful bringing of his tithe."

You see, God will see to it that you receive in the same measure you give.

If your faith is large enough for train loads of offerings, then God will open His heavenly windows large enough for train loads of blessings to be given back to you.

That is His Word!

That is His promise to *you!*

The tithe always *opens the windows* of heaven!

The offering *always determines the measure* of the blessing you get.

Maybe this will explain why so many Christians today are walking around with open windows and empty pockets.

Hold on to your hat as you read the next sentence.

The measure of your blessing that comes through the opened windows of heaven to you is not decided by God, *it is decided by you!*

Remember, to *know* the truth and to apply it in your own life is the thing that will set you free.

Think back with me to the time when you first received your salvation. You were probably so excited in your spirit. You broke through the lies Satan had been feeding you about the "good life" of sin. You may have broken through a circle of friends who were keeping you on the path to destruction. You broke through the lies of atheist schoolteachers, and boldly received Jesus Christ as your Lord and Savior!

You know from experience that breakthroughs are not easy. Real breakthroughs explode violently.

Remember the story about the woman with the issue of blood? She was healed when she touched *the hem* of Christ's garment. The *hem* of Christ's garment was at His feet. That lady crawled on her hands and knees to get her healing. People were probably kicking her, and stepping on her, but she pressed through. She was not moved from her goal by circumstances or by the opinions of others. She did *whatever was necessary* to touch the hem of that garment.

Now, that is a breakthrough!

She stood up, healed, and probably shouted to the crowd, "I've got it! I got my healing."

Forceful people have breakthroughs. Breakthroughs will never come to the timid, or to those not committed to a goal.

Today, you are reading this book to experience a breakthrough. If you are not currently tithing, start right now, and faithfully release your tithe into the work of God.

That will *open* wide the windows of heaven. Then, as you pay your tithe, *get violent.*

Start giving offerings. Not little teaspoon offerings, but generous offerings. Give them boldly in the measure you want them measured back to you again.

I say on the authority of God's Word, and in accordance with what I am seeing from one end of the world to the other, that abundant supply will begin to pour forth from the windows of heaven that your tithe has opened, and when it does, be not deceived. It will flow in the exact measure of your offerings to God.

Child of God, try this process faithfully for at least 120 days, and you will never quit.

12

You May Have To Overcome the Flesh To Give

I feel that some of you may still have doubts about how spiritual the topic of money is. For the few remaining skeptics, let me show you something you probably never noticed about Scripture before.

Many believe that your financial matters are not important to God.

Child of God, let me ask you this question, "If your giving is not important to Jesus, then *why* did He stand and watch the people as they gave during the offerings in the temple?"

You see, Jesus became very aggressive regarding the offering being given in the temple. He watched how much people put in, and then announced when the offerings were generous.

Jesus watched the offering.

> And Jesus sat over against the treasury, and beheld how the people cast money into the treasury: and many that were rich cast in much.
> And there came a certain poor widow, and she threw in two mites, which make a farthing.
> And he called unto him his disciples, and saith unto them, *verily I say unto you, That this poor widow hath cast more in, than all they which have cast into the treasury:*
> *For all they did cast in of their abundance;* but she of her want did cast in all that she had, even all her living.
>
> **Mark 12:41-44**

Child of God, do you see this amazing revelation? Jesus "beheld" the offering. He positioned Himself right near the offering basket and closely *watched* as the people put in their offerings.

Do not tell me Jesus does not care about how much you give! *Jesus does care about your finances!*

He is very fair about your giving. A millionaire can give more money than a poor widow, but the widow will usually give a greater percentage of her money to God than the millionaire will, so God takes into account not only the amount you give, but also the sacrifice you make in the giving.

The widow only gave two mites, but Jesus said this poor widow had cast more in than *all* they who had cast into the treasury.

Why? Because . . .**they** [the rich] **did cast in of their abundance;** the word "abundance" literally means "excess." They gave out of their discretionary income (the portion left after the necessities), *after* the bills were paid.

There is no "discretion" about the rent, you must pay it. There is no choice about the light bill, you must pay it. At this time, the main group of people in the temple were giving out of their discretionary income, that which remained after all the necessary things were paid.

They simply were casually "casting" in their money, money that they did not need to buy vital things for their living.

But the widow gave out of her living. Do not think that this was some little insignificant sum she threw in. Her two mites were more than 25 percent of the amount a Roman soldier was earning in one day. There was buying power in those two mites! They were enough to live on, yet she gave *all* she had — her entire living!

She gave out of her *want.* Notice, the Scripture says her "want," not her need.

What does a poor widow want? We do not know for sure about this particular widow, but there are some things we can speculate about.

She probably just got paid, since laborers were paid daily in those times. As she was coming to the temple with these two mites clutched tightly in her hand, she probably was thinking about what to do with her wages.

Perhaps she would replace the tattered dress of one of her children. Perhaps she would buy beans for the next day's meal.

But not today! The spirit of God moved her during the temple service, and she made a bold decision. She decided to give these two mites to God, to give Him an offering that would provide her with a financial *breakthrough* in her life, an offering that would take her beyond merely having her needs met, and would open to her a new kind of abundance that would also allow her to have her precious wants met.

She probably told herself, "I am sick of living like a pig. I am tired of having crumbs. God, I am going to give to You, and I know You will meet my needs, and even allow me to go beyond my simple needs and let me have my wants also."

So she walked down the temple aisle, inwardly rehearsing all the wants in her life, facing inner conflict all the way up to the last second. Only then did she dare to give *both* of those precious mites to *prove* God. Even then, she had to literally *throw them in* quickly, to keep her needs from overtaking her with their insidious arguments of insufficiency.

The Bible says she violently *threw* in the two mites! No casual "casting" of finances for this widow; she violently *threw* her two mites into the offering, and got her breakthrough!

Child of God, right now I pray you are experiencing a monumental build-up of spiritual energy in your life to receive the new, great anointing God has for you in this area of finances.

You have probably received more knowledge on the subject of Biblical economics from your few hours in this book than you have received on this subject in your entire lifetime.

But knowledge — without application — is not liberating truth. It is only when you *apply* these principles that they become *powerful* enough to break you through from barely having your needs met to the abundant supply of all your wants being met.

> Now unto him that is able to do exceeding abundantly above all *that we ask or think,* according to the *power* that worketh *in us.*
> **Ephesians 3:20**

The widow went for a breakthrough in her finances.

As you start to apply these Biblical principles of economics, I believe *you too* will experience the same type of breakthrough.

It will happen as you *do* two things:

1. Faithfully tithe to open the windows of heaven.

2. Give generous offerings and establish a proper measure for God to use to bless you financially.

Do not wait. Apply these truths in your very next giving opportunity. If this is difficult to do, if fear grips you, you may have to do as the widow did, and you may have to *throw* in your tithe, or *throw* in your offering. You may have to overcome the flesh's apprehension and unbelief with a violent force to enter this new part of the Kingdom of God.

Whatever it takes for you to start, *Do it! Start giving today.*

Do not accept Satan's lies that are designed to try to discourage you and stop your breakthrough. Remember, the offering works for *you* as much as it does for God. It (your offering) determines what measure God can use in pouring out your financial blessing through the *windows* of heaven that your tithe opened wide.

Mark my words, soon there will be a new breed of saints walking the face of the earth. They will not be of the old order, experiencing open windows and empty pockets.

No, they will be a disciplined, obedient army, shouting praise to God, and mightily helping to finance the endtime harvest, as they experience *open windows and overflowing pockets.*

13

Will You Take Your Part in Funding God's Endtime Harvest?

Your hands do have the God-given power to get wealth!

But thou shalt remember the Lord thy God: for it is he that giveth thee power to get wealth, that he may establish his covenant which he sware unto thy fathers, as it is this day.

Deuteronomy 8:18

God intends for this wealth to flow into your control for more reasons than simply supplying you with luxuries (although He does not mind if you have luxuries). Remember, His first miracle was turning water into wine, an undisputed miracle of luxury.

However, He is looking for a new breed of saints with a greater vision than just getting by. They are saints who can envision themselves as major bankers financing the work of God throughout the whole world. They are saints who take their God-given *power* to get wealth, and once they get it, then use that wealth to establish the covenant of God throughout the earth.

And precisely what is God's covenant?

Hundreds of millions of dollars worth of television time has been purchased to discuss the covenant, and most of the preachers discussing it seem to dwell on Deuteronomy 28:8:

The Lord shall command the blessing upon thee in thy storehouses, and in all that thou settest thine

> **hand unto; and he shall bless thee in the land which
> the Lord thy God giveth thee.**

The 28th chapter of Deuteronomy goes on to say that you are the head, not the tail; you are above and not beneath; you will be blessed in your basket; you will be blessed in the city.

Blessed. Blessed. Blessed. Blessed. Child of God, *that is* not the covenant! Those are the *blessings* of the covenant! Here is the covenant in its shortest, plainest form:

> **And I will make of thee a great nation, and I will
> bless thee, and make thy name great; and thou shalt
> be a blessing:**

> **And I will bless them that bless thee, and curse
> him that curseth thee: and in thee shall all families
> of the earth be blessed.**

> **Genesis 12:2,3**

God first promises to bless you — so you can be a blessing to others! *That is* the covenant. *Blessed to bless.* And how can you best be a blessing to others? By bringing them the salvation message of Jesus Christ. Now notice the Godly progression. Yes, God does clearly intend for you to be blessed. But the covenant does not stop there.

God *then* intends for you to take *your* blessings and pass them on to others — starting with the saving message of Jesus! God is looking for a select group of endtime saints who clearly understand His covenant, so that He can abundantly bless them, and they in turn can liberally turn the wealth (God has given them the power to get) towards financing the final, endtime harvest of this world.

Make no mistake about it: the wealth *for* that final harvest is already in the world, and now it is up to you and me to begin to fulfill a series of prophecies that are clear in God's Word.

> **The wealth of the sinner** [wicked] **is laid up for the just.**
>
> **Proverbs 13:22b**

Step by step and bit by bit, God is going to begin the most amazing transfer of the world's wealth in the history of man. You have already seen that such a transfer is consistent with God's nature through God's Word. You know about the miracle transfer of wealth that took place as Israel came out of Egyptian bondage. You also know how God abundantly funded and mobilized His church during the reign of Constantine.

Even the closely guarded money of banks, and other excessive interest-charging institutions, as well as any money that has been unjustly taken, will be included as part of this vast divine transfer of monies from wicked hands into the hands of those who pity the poor.

> **He that by usury and unjust gain increaseth his substance, he shall gather it for him that will pity the poor.**
>
> **Proverbs 28:8**

Why will God give all this wealth to Christians? Because God knows that His good stewards will give this wealth to improve the lowly status of the poor, and that further, these stewards will "bless" the poor with the salvation message of Jesus.

All of these years, Christians have been lamenting, "Lord, Lord, why are you letting all of these wicked men become rich?" "Dear God, how long will interest rates continue to soar?" Well, *now* we know the answer.

God has given the wicked men of this world a ministry. God has commissioned them to heap up their riches over their lifetime so that He can use it for His endtime plan.

> **For God giveth to a man that is good in his sight wisdom, and knowledge, and joy: but to the sinner he giveth travail, to gather and to heap up, that he may give to him that is good before God.**
> **Ecclesiastes 2:26a**

Isn't God amazing? Every day, these rich men are out there working, deceiving, abandoning their families, ignoring the rules, risking prison — just to build their fortunes! And now, God has a message of travail for them, their wealth is already in the process of undergoing a worldwide transfer. Look at Job 27, 13, 16, 17:

> **This is the portion of a wicked man with God, and the heritage of oppressors, which they shall receive of the Almighty.**
>
> **Though he heap up silver as the dust, and prepare raiment as the clay;**
>
> **He [the wicked man] may prepare it, but the just shall put it on, and the innocent shall divide the silver.**

God is going to take the silver from the wealthy wicked, and He is going to hand that silver, and the monies of the unsaved bankers, and the oil riches of the Arabs, and the money in the International Monetary Fund — *all* over to the "innocent" for the funding of His final endtime harvest! Remember, He gives us power to get wealth so that the covenant (His promises to bless all families of the world) can be established.

God always fulfills His Word, even when what it says seems impossible to men. He said a virgin would conceive a child, and as impossible as that sounds, she did.

Now God is declaring the wealth of the wicked will begin transferring over to the innocent — and as impossible as that seems, it will surely happen. This message of wealth transfer literally runs throughout all of Scripture.

> **But ye shall be named the Priests of the Lord: men shall call you the ministers of our God:** *ye shall eat the riches of the Gentiles,* **and in their glory shall ye boast yourselves.**
>
> **Isaiah 61:6**

You and I will "eat the riches of the Gentiles" (those who do not know Jesus Christ as Savior)! As the "ministers" of God, He has made available to us as part of our inheritance the very wealth of the wicked.

> **There is an evil** [a distressing thing] **which I have seen under the sun, and it is common among men** [it happens all the time!]:
>
> **A man to whom God hath given riches, wealth, and honour, so that he wanteth nothing for his soul of all that he desireth, yet God giveth him not power to eat thereof, but a stranger eateth it.**
>
> **Ecclesiastes 6:1,2a**

Child of God, who is the "stranger" to a rich, wicked man? I boldly declare that it is you and I — the saints of God. There is no fellowship between the money hungry power merchants of the world and the

Christians. They are *total strangers* to each other! Yet, God says they will not for long partake of their wealth, but that "a stranger," someone unknown to them, will take control of it.

Time after time, throughout history, God has allowed vast sums of money, silver, gold, and other possessions to transfer from the wicked to the just. Isaac experienced such a great transformation of wealth that the wicked Philistines envied him.

The Israelites left the bondage of Egypt equipped with gold, silver, food, and clothing, provided by the same Egyptians who had been their wealthy, wicked masters just a few hours before!

Jacob served Laban under the most impossible wage compensation program ever devised, yet Jacob still took control of Laban's wealth.

Most of the wealth of the Roman Empire was transferred to the saints of God during the time of Constantine, when all of Rome was converted to Christianity.

The transformation of the wealth of the wicked to the just has happened before, and it will happen again!

Abundance is overdue. I am tired of hearing poverty-stricken Christians say, "I used to be a wealthy person, flying around the country in my private jet, but praise God, I lost all of that. My home is gone, my factory is destroyed, my plain was repossessed, and now I live in a one-room, rented apartment. Praise God, I am delivered."

Do not misunderstand; their salvation is glorious. But why do they always have to lose the factory and the jet plane? It is time for the church to start hearing testimonies that say, "Yes, I got saved, and I still have the Lear jet, and I did own a million dollar home before I got saved, and I still have it now that I am saved. Yes, I did spend a great sum of money on sinful things when I was lost, but now I spend even more on the Gospel. I recently gave six million dollars to help provide 24-hour-a-day television for India, and now millions of lost souls there are accepting Jesus as their Savior. And, after I gave that six million dollars, the Lord blessed another business venture I was culminating, and blessed me with an eighteen million dollar profit. Praise God! With this money, we will be paying off all the debts of every gospel-preaching church in our city."

That is a testimony! Please do not think that this is impossible. King David paid for the building of the entire temple at Jerusalem with money he took from wicked heathens. He was a king with a great harvest to bring in for God. According to Scripture, *you* are a king with a great harvest to bring in. According to Scripture, the Old Testament saints were to be examples to us. God did it before, and He is starting to do it again.

The Key Verse to This Revelation

Read the following verse very closely. It is the *key verse of this book.* Let it sink into your spirit, for it clearly tells us *when* the next great worldwide transference of wealth from the wicked heathen to the saved will take place.

Go to now, ye rich men, weep and howl for your miseries that shall come upon you.

> **Your riches are corrupted, and your garments are motheaten.**
>
> **Your gold and silver is cankered; and the rust of them shall be a witness against you, and shall eat your flesh as it were fire.** *Ye have heaped treasure together for the last days.*
>
> **James 5:1-3**

After reading that last verse, can you feel a special surge of spiritual energy beginning to work in you? Child of God, believe me, you will need this kind of energy to make your violent breakthrough, and for you to begin to take control of the wealth of the wicked.

Let us look closely at this passage. What makes the wicked rich weep and howl with sorrow? Is it when their spouses leave them? Of course not. Many rich men and women insist that their new spouse sign prenuptial agreements to protect their vast riches at the time of their sure-to-come divorce!

Do wicked rich weep and howl over their children going bad? Not for very long. The wicked rich just send their problem children away with credit cards and the message, "Don't call us, we'll call you. Just get out of my life, and I'll pay your bills."

The thing that moves the wicked rich to weeping and howling is when their money goes from their control! *That's* what causes them to weep and howl.

Right now, these wicked rich men and women have once again come to the day of their weeping and howling because this Scripture clearly says that it is for *the last days* that they are stacking up their wealth.

Please notice, this is not speaking of retirement plans. This is not speaking of anything that the wicked wealthy even realize they are doing. It is not a part of the wicked wealthy philosophy to believe in Biblical endtime prophecies. They view the Bible teachings on the endtimes as myth.

That is why this portion of Scripture is revelatory. James reveals why the rich are so determined to stack up money and treasure: it is something that is beyond their own control. They are *compulsively* gathering their wealth *for the last days!*

> **For God giveth to a man that is good in his sight wisdom, and knowledge, and joy: but to the sinner he giveth travail, *to gather and to heap up, that* he may give to him that is good before God.**
> **Ecclesiastes 2:26a**

Through prayer and study, God gave me this revelation just as though I were standing in the throne room of God, listening to Him. And now He is sending me with this special revelation to the Church to bring the good news *that the wealth of the wicked is now ready to be taken!*

Have you ever noticed how rich people just cannot seem to get enough money? If you know a wicked millionaire, there's never a problem knowing what to give him for Christmas.

Give him more money, and you will be giving him his heart's desire. The wicked rich man never has so much that he does not want more. If he has two million, then he wants to try to get four. If he has eight million, he wants to get ten. If he has two hundred million, then he wants a billion. If he has a billion, then he wants two billion. He will die before his hunger for wealth is ever satisfied.

In the mid-Sixties, when I was a pastor in Denver, Colorado, the local paper carried a story about a little woman who died on skid row. When they took her body off the bed, they saw huge lumps in her dirty mattress. When they unzipped the mattress, much to their surprise, the mattress was full of — you guessed it — money!

Then they spotted holes in the walls near the ceiling, and when they looked into these holes, they found the cavities between the studs of the walls were full of money. For decades, this little woman had been going out, collecting pop bottles, gathering junk, to turn into money. She had money in the bed, in the walls, in the ceiling, and under the floor — hundreds of thousands of dollars.

When the cause of her death was determined, everyone was amazed, for she died of malnutrition. She starved to death. Her greed grew to the point where she could not even take one single dollar from her wall and go out and buy a cup of milk to drink.

That is how compulsive the drive to accumulate money can become! But strange as this compulsion for gathering and heaping up money may seem, it is within God's plan, for He puts it into the heart of the wicked to gather and lay up for the funding of His endtime plan in the final harvest. (Eccl. 2:26.)

Every day, the wealthy wicked are taking the money out of circulation. They are hoarding it in their safe deposit boxes and in Swiss bank accounts.

Now, perhaps you can begin to better understand why these things are happening. Unknown to them, these men are gathering money for a definite purpose, a purpose beyond their own knowledge. *They are gathering it to give to those who are good before God!*

Child of God, this is a message for you. God has a plan for funding His church, and this same plan will also fund your needs and wants.

If you are walking in ignorance, if you do not know God's intentions for your life as it relates to financing the end time harvest, you will miss His plan and you will surely miss *your part* in financing the endtime harvest.

Balancing your budget is not enough. Simply tithing is not enough. You now know that your tithes are not going to bring you the surplus that you need for satisfying your craving to fund the ministries God is laying on your heart.

Your tithing establishes with God that you are a faithful, trustworthy honest steward, thereby *opening the windows* of heaven to you.

Do not forget this most imporant part: it is your offerings that determine *the measure* of the abundance that will flow through those open windows.

Today, we need a group of saints with faith enough to rise up with strong *offerings,* and give not in teaspoons, or cup measures, but in large abundant measures, bringing the potential of the full measure of Luke 6:38 into full operation in their lives.

> **Give, and it shall be given unto you; good measure, pressed down, and shaken together, and running over, shall men give unto your bosom. *For with the same measure that ye mete withal, it shall be measured to you again.***
>
> **Luke 6:38**

Strange as it may seem to you, as much as it fights against what you have been taught, God's financial abundance in your life is decided by *you and you alone!*

If you want to receive larger blessings, increase the measure of your offerings to God. Break through from giving cupfuls and begin giving shovelfuls.

It is time for you to take this new Biblical information that you have received from this book and let it energize you to break away from the old concepts you learned about finances; concepts learned from your parents, your Bible school teachers, and for many, even your well-meaning pastors, into total obedience to God's Word on Biblical economics.

It is a new day for a new breed of saints to seize the finances God has for them, even the finances of the wicked wealthy, not just for your own personal blessing, but true abundance in finances so that you can become a blessing to others!

Remember, this will not come easy. You will have to want to change your current financial status as badly as the woman with the issue of blood wanted to change her physical condition. *She crawled* through a crowd to touch the hem of His garment.

You have to want this financial breakthrough as badly as the widow who gave her last bit of meal to God's prophet, and then was blessed by God with food throughout the entire famine.

You have to want it as badly as the widow who *threw* two mites into the temple offering. She violently said to herself: "I've had it with my life the way it is. I want a breakthrough. I want my life to change." She put in her living expense money.

Now, child of God, don't take my word for this, take God's Word on it. That widow became violent, and she took the Kingdom by force.

If a man were physically harming your wife or family, you would not politely ask him to stop. You would become violent. You would use every available thing in your grasp to stop him. You would not stop fighting until your wife and family were safe.

Today, Satan is in full attack against the finances of so many of the saints of God. He is brutalizing many of them, taking food from babies, and removing much needed necessities from many of God's children.

Friend of mine, *it is time for you to become violent.* It is time to yell, "No, you can't take any more of the money God intends for me. You can't keep me from the riches God intends for me to control for Him. I'm going to take the wealth of the wicked and use it for God's intended purpose, to finance a worldwide harvest that will complete a Kingdom that will never end. So Satan, I put you on notice that *I am getting violent!"*

Child of God, spiritual violence is the key to your breakthrough. God wrote down the examples of the men and women of the Bible you have studied about in this book to make your victory easier through their example. Isn't it wonderful that the Bible is alive and vibrant for you today?

Now you are ready for the breakthrough. This is your day for a new beginning.

You are living in a specific time, and you can experience the specific fulfillment of this endtime revelation. God wants to transfer the wealth of the wicked into your hands. The psalmist saw the unfolding of James 5:1-3 when he wrote, under God's anointing:

> For I was envious at the foolish, when I saw the prosperity of the wicked.
>
> Psalm 73:3

In verse 17, God reveals the overall picture:

> Until I went into the sanctuary of God; then understood I their end.
>
> Psalm 73:17

What end did the prophet see in the sanctuary of God? That the wicked's wealth was soon to be snatched from them!

If you want to start reaping your part of this endtime inheritance, then start sowing as never before. The widows had to sow first. Sow your precious seed, and God will return it back to you in the same measure you gave to Him.

> They that sow in tears [hard times] shall reap in joy.
>
> He that goeth forth and weepeth, bearing *precious seed* [the last seed from the bottom of the barrel], shall *doubtless* [without question] come again with rejoicing, bringing his sheaves [the increase of the harvest] with him.
>
> Psalm 126:5,6

Notice carefully God's promise here: When you sow, you *shall doubtless* return with sheaves (the increase of the harvest).

That is not a matter of luck, it is a matter of spiritual obedience to spiritual law. When you give to God's work, He will honor His Word and He will cause men to give back to you in like measure. The cycle for God's endtime harvest is here, the wonderful time God spoke of when He said:

> **And I will shake all nations, and the desire of all nations shall come: and I will fill this house with glory, saith the Lord of hosts.**
>
> *The silver is mine, and the gold is mine,* **saith the Lord of hosts.**
>
> **The glory of this latter house shall be greater than of the former, saith the Lord of hosts: and in this place will I give peace, saith the Lord of hosts.**
>
> **Haggai 2:7-9**

No matter whose name is on the real estate deed, no matter whose name is behind the billion dollar numbered Swiss bank account, the Bible says that the silver and the gold belong to God. He intends for the saints of today to have that wealth — so the glory of His endtime house (the church of God, a holy temple, not made with human hands) will be great.

— Greater than the glory of Jacob when he departed, prosperous and loaded with wealth, after his employment with Laban.

— Greater than the glory of Israel when they left Egypt, overflowing with gold, silver, clothing, and food.

— Greater than the glory of the chuch of Constantine's day when every corner of the earth was evangelized.

Child of God, this transfer of the wealth of the wicked begins with *you* and your decisive actions. The saints must first individually put the Biblical principles of economics to work in their lives — *then* the endtime revelation will begin to materialize.

No one could stand in your place for your salvation. You made the decision, and *you* took the action, and you received the promise — life everlasting.

The same is true of your finances. No one can receive God's abundance for you. *You* must first make the decision, based upon the Biblical understanding you have received in this book, and then, *you* must *open* your own wallet, and *give to the Gospel*, thus planting the proper seed that will allow God's abundance to begin to flow into your life.

God wants you to participate in His endtime redistribution of the wealth of the wicked. He wants you to have a part in the redistribution of that wealth into ministries that will bless every family of the earth with the Gospel of Jesus Christ, fulfilling His covenant.

> **And I will make of thee a great nation, and I will bless thee, and make thy name great; and *thou shalt be a blessing.***
>
> **And I will bless them that bless thee, and curse him that curseth thee: and *in thee shall all families of the earth be blessed.***
>
> **Genesis 12:2,3**

The decision to participate in this process is in your hands. *You are needed* by God to help finance the final, endtime harvest. He is waiting on your decision, and your action.

You now know what God's Word says about the wealth of the wicked. You now know that God has definite plans for their finances, to use them to bless your life abundantly, so you can abundantly bless others. You now know that these key Biblical principles of economics will allow your tithes and offerings to work as God fully intended them to work.

You have concentrated knowledge of God's endtime plan as it pertains to finances and that knowledge, when *acted upon*, will bring you *great* financial power.

Right now, trust the Holy Spirit to work in your life, and say this prayer out loud:

"Father, in the name of Jesus, I come into Your presence, and thank You for the truths You have taught me in this book, *truths that are taken directly from your word.*

"I am willing to obey You, and I declare in faith that this is a *new day of financial freedom for me.* I commit myself before You and Your angels to put into action Your biblical principles of economics. I promise to *faithfully tithe,* and *give generous offerings* which will enable abundance to start flowing into my life.

"I will tithe first before I pay any other bill, and I will use a generous portion of my finances to give to those ministries that preach the Gospel around the world.

"Then, according to Your purpose, I will use a reasonable portion of the finances You supply to purchase the things I need and want, knowing *as I seek your kingdom and your righteousness first,* You *will see to it that all these things that I need and want will be abundantly added to me.*

"Lord God, I thank You for revealing Yourself to me through this book, and in the name of Jesus, *I bind Satan from any further interference in my finances.* In the name of Jesus, I loose Your abundant blessings in my finances, and in my life. Amen."

Now, child of God, go boldly where many others have gone before. Go in the steps of Abraham, Isaac, Jacob — men who took the wealth of the wicked according to the promise of God.

Go boldly into this new day and put the ax to the root of the corrupt tree of the world's finances, and bring these finances (the world's wealth) into captivity for our Lord and Savior Jesus Christ, to be freely used to win to Him the very wicked that the wealth came from!

> **And the wealth of the sinner is laid up for the just.**
>
> **Proverbs 13:22b**